GCSE
Success

WORKBOOK

Maths
Higher Tier

Fiona Mapp

Contents

Number

Revised

Algebra

Revised

Contents

Contents

3

Homework diary

TOPIC	SCORE
Fractions	/36
Approximations & using a calculator	/29
Percentages 1	/36
Percentages 2	/36
Fractions, decimals & percentages	/28
Recurring decimals & surds	/55
Ratio	/32
Indices	/47
Standard index form	/37
Upper & lower bounds of measurement	/30
Algebra & formulae	/41
Equations	/43
Equations & inequalities	/36
Advanced algebra & equations	/40
Direct & inverse proportion	/38
Straight-line graphs	/21
Curved graphs	/24
Advanced graphs	/24
Interpreting graphs	/22
Bearings & scale drawings	/25
Transformations 1	/22
Transformations 2	/21
Similarity & congruency	/24
Loci & coordinates in 3D	/17
Angle properties of circles	/23
Pythagoras' theorem	/31
Trigonometry in right-angled triangles	/31
Application of trigonometry	/34
Further trigonometry	/43
Measures & measurement	/39
Area of 2D shapes	/32
Volume of 3D shapes	/35
Further length, area & volume	/31
Vectors	/28
Collecting data	/17
Scatter graphs & correlation	/22
Averages 1	/27
Averages 2	/24
Cumulative frequency graphs	/25
Histograms	/14
Probability	/29

Revision & exam tips

Planning and revising:

- Mathematics should be revised **actively**. You should be doing **more than just reading**.
- Find out the dates of your first mathematics examination. Make an examination and revision timetable.
- After completing a topic in school, go through the topic again in the **GCSE Success Revision Guide**. Copy out the **main points, results** and **formulae** into a notebook or use a **highlighter** to emphasise them.
- Try to write out the **key points** from **memory**. Check what you have written and see if there are any differences.
- Revise in short bursts of about **30 minutes**, followed by a **short break**.
- Learn **facts** from your exercise books, notebooks and the **Success Revision Guide**. **Memorise** any formulae you need to learn.
- Learn with a friend to make it easier and more fun!
- Do the **multiple-choice** and **short-answer** questions in this book and check your answers to see how much you know.
- Once you feel **confident** that you know the topic, do the **GCSE-style** questions in this book. **Highlight** the key words in the question, **plan** your answer and then go back and **check** that you have answered the question.
- **Make a note** of any topics that you do not understand and **go back through** the notes again.

Different types of questions:

- On the **GCSE Mathematics papers** you will have several types of questions:
  Calculate – In these questions you need to work out the answer. Remember that it is important to show full working out.
  Explain – These questions want you to explain, with a mathematical reason or calculation, what the answer is.
  Show – These questions usually require you to show, with mathematical justification, what the answer is.
  Write down or state – These questions require no explanation or working out.
  Prove – These questions want you to set out a concise logical argument, making the reasons clear.
  Deduce – These questions make use of an earlier answer to establish a result.

On the day:

- **Follow the instructions** on the exam paper. Make sure that you understand what any **symbols** mean.
- Make sure that you **read the question** carefully so that you give the answer that an examiner wants.
- Always **show your working**; you may pick up some marks even if your final answer is wrong.
- Do **rough calculations** to check your answers and make sure that they are **reasonable**.
- When carrying out a calculation, **do not round the answer until the end**, otherwise your final answer will not be as accurate as is needed.
- Lay out your working **carefully** and **concisely**. Write down the calculations that you are going to make. You usually get marks for showing a **correct method**.
- Make your drawings and graphs **neat** and **accurate**.
- Know what is on the **formulae page** and make sure that you **learn** those formulae that are not on it.
- If you cannot do a question, **leave it out** and **go back** to it at the end.
- Keep an eye on the time. Allow enough time to check through your answers.
- If you finish early, check through everything very carefully and try to fill in any gaps.
- Try to write something even if you are not sure about it. Leaving an empty space will score you no marks.

Good luck!

Fractions

Multiple-choice questions

Choose just one answer, a, b, c or d. Circle your choice.

1 In a class of 24 students, $\frac{3}{8}$ wear glasses. How many students wear glasses?

    a) 9   **b)** 6   **c)** 3   **d)** 12   **(1 mark)**

2 Which one of these fractions is equivalent to $\frac{5}{9}$?

    a) $\frac{16}{27}$ **b)** $\frac{9}{18}$ **c)** $\frac{25}{45}$ **d)** $\frac{21}{36}$ **(1 mark)**

3 Work out the answer to $1\frac{5}{9} - \frac{1}{3}$

    a) $\frac{1}{3}$ **b)** $1\frac{2}{9}$ **c)** $1\frac{4}{6}$ **d)** $\frac{4}{12}$ **(1 mark)**

4 Work out the answer to $\frac{2}{11} \times \frac{7}{9}$

    a) $\frac{14}{11}$ **b)** $\frac{14}{9}$ **c)** $\frac{14}{99}$ **d)** $\frac{2}{99}$ **(1 mark)**

5 Work out the answer to $\frac{3}{10} \div \frac{2}{3}$

    a) $\frac{9}{20}$ **b)** $\frac{6}{50}$ **c)** $\frac{6}{15}$ **d)** $\frac{4}{3}$ **(1 mark)**

Score / 5

Short-answer questions

Answer all parts of each question.

1 State whether these statements are **true** or **false**.

    a) $\frac{4}{5}$ of 20 is bigger than $\frac{6}{7}$ of 14. _____ **(1 mark)**

    b) $\frac{2}{9}$ of 27 is smaller than $\frac{1}{3}$ of 15. _____ **(1 mark)**

2 In a class of 32 pupils, $\frac{1}{8}$ are left-handed. How many students are not left-handed?

_____ **(1 mark)**

3 Work out the answers to the following. Give your answers in the simplest form.

    a) $\frac{2}{9} + \frac{1}{3}$ _____   **b)** $\frac{7}{11} - \frac{1}{4}$ _____   **c)** $\frac{4}{7} \times \frac{3}{8}$ _____

    d) $\frac{9}{12} \div \frac{1}{4}$ _____   **e)** $2\frac{5}{7} - 1\frac{1}{21}$ _____   **f)** $\frac{4}{9} + \frac{3}{27}$ _____

    g) $\frac{7}{12} \times 1\frac{1}{2}$ _____   **h)** $1\frac{4}{7} \div \frac{7}{12}$ _____   **(8 marks)**

4 Arrange these fractions in order of size, **smallest** first.

    a) $\frac{2}{3}$ $\frac{4}{5}$ $\frac{1}{7}$ $\frac{3}{4}$ $\frac{1}{2}$ $\frac{3}{10}$

_____ **(2 marks)**

    b) $\frac{5}{8}$ $\frac{1}{3}$ $\frac{2}{7}$ $\frac{1}{9}$ $\frac{3}{4}$ $\frac{2}{5}$

_____ **(2 marks)**

Score / 15

Answer all parts of the questions. Show your workings (on a separate sheet of paper if necessary) and include the correct units in your answers.

1 Work out the following:

a) $\frac{2}{7} \times \frac{4}{9}$ _____ (1 mark)

b) $3\frac{9}{11} - 2\frac{1}{3}$ _____ (2 marks)

2 Charlotte's take-home pay is £930. She gives her mother $\frac{1}{3}$ of this and spends $\frac{1}{5}$ of the £930 on going out. What fraction of the £930 is left? Give your answer in its simplest form.

_____

_____ (3 marks)

3 Phoebe says, 'Since 5 is halfway between 4 and 6, then $\frac{1}{5}$ will be halfway between $\frac{1}{4}$ and $\frac{1}{6}$.' Phoebe is wrong. Show that $\frac{1}{5}$ is not halfway between $\frac{1}{4}$ and $\frac{1}{6}$.

_____

_____ (3 marks)

4 Molly wins some money on the lottery. She uses $\frac{1}{3}$ of her lottery win to buy a house and she gives $\frac{1}{8}$ of her lottery win to charity. Molly then shares the remainder of her lottery win equally among her four children. Work out the fraction of Molly's lottery win that each of her four children receives.

_____

_____ (4 marks)

5 Thomas shares a bag of 30 sweets with his friends. He gives Jessica $\frac{2}{5}$ of his sweets and he gives Samuel $\frac{1}{6}$ of his sweets. He keeps the rest for himself. How many sweets does Thomas keep for himself?

Sweets

_____

_____ (3 marks)

Score   / 16

How well did you do?

| 0–12 | Try again | 13–19 | Getting there | 20–27 | Good work | 28–36 | Excellent! |

For more information on this topic, see pages 10–11 of your Success Revision Guide.

Number

Approximations & using a calculator

Number

Multiple-choice questions

Choose just one answer, a, b, c or d. Circle your choice.

1 Estimate the answer to the calculation 27×41.

   a) 1107   **b)** 1200   **c)** 820   **d)** 1300   (1 mark)

2 A carton of orange juice costs 79p. Estimate the cost of 402 cartons of orange juice.

   a) £350   **b)** £250   **c)** £400   **d)** £320   (1 mark)

3 A school trip is organised. 396 pupils are going on the trip. Each coach seats 50 pupils. Approximately how many coaches are needed?

   a) 12   **b)** 5   **c)** 8   **d)** 10   (1 mark)

4 Estimate the answer to the calculation $\frac{(4.2)^2}{107}$

   a) 16   **b)** 1.6   **c)** 0.16   **d)** 160   (1 mark)

5 Round 5379 to 3 significant figures.

   a) 538   **b)** 5370   **c)** 537   **d)** 5380   (1 mark)

Score   / 5

Short-answer questions

Answer all parts of each question.

1 State whether each statement is **true** or **false**.

   a) 2.742 rounded to 3 significant figures is 2.74   (1 mark)

   b) 2793 rounded to 2 significant figures is 27   (1 mark)

   c) 32 046 rounded to 1 significant figure is 40 000   (1 mark)

   d) 14.637 rounded to 3 significant figures is 14.6   (1 mark)

2 Work out the following. Give your answers to 3 significant figures. 🖩

   a) $\frac{4.2 \times (3.6 + 5.1)}{2 - 1.9}$ **b)** $6 \times \sqrt{\frac{12.1}{4.2}}$

   c) $\frac{12^5}{4.3 \times 9.15}$ **d)** $\frac{4\cos 30° + 2\sin 60°}{4^3}$ (4 marks)

3 Round each of the numbers in the following calculations to 1 significant figure, then work out an approximate answer.

   a) $\frac{(32.9)^2}{9.1}$

      (1 mark)

   b) $\frac{(906 \div 31.4)^2}{7.1 + 2.9}$

      (1 mark)

Score   / 10

GCSE-style questions

Answer all parts of the questions. Show your workings (on a separate sheet of paper if necessary) and include the correct units in your answers.

1 The highest mountains on each continent are shown in the table below.

Mountain peak	Continent	Height (m)
Mount Everest	Asia	8850
Aconcagua	South America	6959
Mount McKinley	North America	6194
Kilimanjaro	Africa	5895
Mount Elbrus	Europe	5642
Vinson Massif	Antarctica	4897
Carstensz Pyramid	Oceania	4884

a) Which two mountains would have the same height if their heights were rounded to 2 significant figures?

....

(1 mark)

b) Gareth says, 'The difference in height between Mount Everest and Carstensz Pyramid is about 4000m.' Is Gareth correct? Give a reason for your answer.

....

....

(2 marks)

2 a) Use your calculator to work out the value of the following. Write down all the figures on your calculator display. 🖩

$$\frac{27.1 \times 6.2}{38.2 - 9.9}$$

(2 marks)

b) Round each of the numbers in the above calculation to 1 significant figure and obtain an approximate answer.

....

(3 marks)

3 a) Use your calculator to work out the value of the following. Write down all the figures on your calculator display. 🖩

$$\frac{(15.2 + 6.9)^2}{3.63 - 4.2}$$

(2 marks)

b) Round your answer to 3 significant figures.

....

(1 mark)

4 Estimate the answer to the following. Leave your answer as an improper fraction in its simplest form.

$$\frac{21.2^2 + 10.3^2}{3.6 \times 2.9}$$

(3 marks)

Score   / 14

How well did you do?

| 0–8 | Try again | 9–17 | Getting there | 18–23 | Good work | 24–29 | Excellent! |

For more information on this topic, see pages 5 and 14–15 of your Success Revision Guide.

Percentages 1

Multiple-choice questions

Choose just one answer, a, b, c or d. Circle your choice.

1. Work out 10% of £850.

   a) £8.50   b) £0.85   c) £85   d) £42.50   (1 mark)

2. Work out 17.5% of £60.

   a) £9   b) £15   c) £10.50   d) £12.50   (1 mark)

3. In a survey, 17 people out of 25 said they preferred type A cola. What percentage of people preferred type A cola?

   a) 68%   b) 60%   c) 72%   d) 75%   (1 mark)

4. A CD player costs £60 in a sale after a reduction of 20%. What was the original price of the CD player? 🖩

   a) £48   b) £70   c) £72   d) £75   (1 mark)

5. A new car was bought for £15 000. Two years later it was sold for £12 000. What is the percentage loss?

   a) 25%   b) 20%   c) 80%   d) 70%   (1 mark)

Score   / 5

Short-answer questions

Answer all parts of each question.

1. Work out the answers to the following:

   a) 20% of £90 _____   b) 30% of £150 _____

   c) 5% of £80 _____   d) 12.5% of 40g _____   (4 marks)

2. Last year, Colin earned £25 500. This year he has a 3% pay rise. How much does Colin now earn? 🖩

   (2 marks)

3. 12 out of 30 people wear glasses. What percentage wear glasses? 🖩

   (2 marks)

4. Lucinda scored 58 out of 75 in a test. What percentage did she get, correct to 1 decimal place? 🖩

   (2 marks)

5. The cost of a ticket for a pop concert has risen by 15% to £23. What was the original price of the ticket? 🖩

   (2 marks)

6 The price of a games console has been reduced by 20% in a sale. It now costs £180. What was the original price? 📱

_____ (2 marks)

7 A coat costs £140. In a sale it is reduced to £85. What is the percentage reduction? Give your answer to 3 significant figures. 📱

_____ (2 marks)

Score   / 16

GCSE-style questions

Answer all parts of the questions. Show your workings (on a separate sheet of paper if necessary) and include the correct units in your answers.

1 Briony wants to calculate what percentage of her annual salary she spends on petrol for her car in one year. Using the following information, calculate this percentage. 📱

Average mileage = 610 miles per month
Fuel consumption = 8 miles per litre
Price of fuel = 103.4p per litre
Annual salary = £18 372

_____ %   (6 marks)

2 Richard is buying a car for £8250. He pays a 20% deposit and then takes out a loan for the rest of the payment. The loan is charged at an interest rate of 7% per year. Richard intends to pay back the loan in one year. How much does Richard pay in total for the car? 📱

£ _____   (3 marks)

3 A car is bought for £17 900. Two years later it is sold for £14 320. Work out the percentage loss. 📱

_____ %   (3 marks)

4 In a sale, all normal prices are reduced by 18%. In the sale, Suki pays £57.40 for a jacket. Calculate the normal price of the jacket. 📱

£ _____   (3 marks)

Score   / 15

How well did you do?

| 0–9 | Try again | 10–19 | Getting there | 20–29 | Good work | 30–36 | Excellent! |

Number

For more information on this topic, see pages 16–19 of your Success Revision Guide.

11

Percentages 2

Multiple-choice questions

Choose just one answer, a, b, c or d. Circle your choice.

1 £2000 is invested in a savings account. Compound interest is paid at 2.1% p.a. How much interest will have been paid after two years? 🔲

   a) £4   **b)** £5.20   **c)** £2.44   **d)** £84.88   (1 mark)

2 A bike was bought for £120. Each year it depreciated in value by 10%. What was the bike worth two years later? 🔲

   a) £97.20   **b)** £98   **c)** £216   **d)** £110   (1 mark)

3 Roberto has £5000 in his savings account. Simple interest is paid at 3% p.a. How much does he have in his savings account at the end of the year? 🔲

   a) £4850   **b)** £5010   **c)** £5150   **d)** £5140.50   (1 mark)

4 Lily earns £23 500. National Insurance (NI) is deducted at 11%. How much NI must she pay? 🔲

   a) £2250   **b)** £2585   **c)** £2605   **d)** £21 385   (1 mark)

Score   / 4

Short-answer questions

Answer all parts of each question.

1 VAT of 5% is added to a gas bill of £72. Calculate the total amount to be paid.

(2 marks)

2 A motorbike is bought for £9000. Each year it depreciates in value by 12%. Work out the value of the motorbike after two years. 🔲

(2 marks)

3 Scarlett has £6200 in her savings account. If compound interest is paid at 2.7% p.a., how much interest will she have earned in total after three years? 🔲

(2 marks)

4 A house was bought for £112 000. After the first year the price had increased by 8%; during the second year it increased by a further 12%. What is the house now worth to the nearest pound? 🔲

(2 marks)

5 Petrol cost 103.9 pence per litre. The price increased by 2%. Six months later it increased again, by 5%. How much does a litre of petrol now cost? Give your answer to 1 decimal place. 🔲

                                                          p

(2 marks)

Score   / 10

Answer all parts of the questions. Show your workings (on a separate sheet of paper if necessary) and include the correct units in your answers.

1 In a sale, a shop took 20% off normal prices. On 'Terrific Tuesday', it took a further 20% off its sale prices. Bibi says, 'That means there was 40% off the normal prices.' Bibi is wrong. Explain why. 🖩

(2 marks)

2 William invests £2000 in each of two bank accounts. The terms of the bank accounts are shown below.

Super Savers	**Nest Egg**
Simple interest at 4% per annum	Compound interest at 4% per annum

Work out the difference between the two bank accounts in the amount of interest that William receives at the end of two years. 🖩

(4 marks)

3 £7000 is invested for three years at 6% compound interest. Work out the total interest earned over the three years. 🖩

(3 marks)

4 This year a company director paid £37 246 tax at the higher rate of 40%. Next year the higher rate of tax will increase to 50%. If the company director's salary stays the same, how much will she pay in tax at the new higher rate? 🖩

(4 marks)

5 Sara bought a car for £14 000. Each year the value of the car depreciated by 10%. Work out the value of the car two years after she bought it.

(3 marks)

6 Nigel invests £7000 for three years at 4% compound interest. How much is Nigel's investment worth after three years? 🖩

(3 marks)

7 A vintage bottle of champagne was valued at £42 000 on 1 January this year. The value of the champagne is predicted to increase at a rate of R% per annum. The predicted value, £V, of the champagne after n years is given by the formula $V = 42\,000 \times (1.045)^n$

a) Write down the value of R. (1 mark)

b) Find the predicted value of the champagne after eight years. 🖩

(2 marks)

Score   / 22

How well did you do?

| 0–8 | Try again | 9–16 | Getting there | 17–27 | Good work | 28–36 | Excellent! |

For more information on this topic, see pages 16–19 of your Success Revision Guide.

Number

Fractions, decimals & percentages

Multiple-choice questions

Choose just one answer, a, b, c or d. Circle your choice.

1 What is $\frac{3}{5}$ as a percentage?

  a) 30%   **b)** 25%   **c)** 60%   **d)** 75%   (1 mark)

2 What is $\frac{2}{3}$ written as a decimal?

  a) 0.77   **b)** $0.\dot{6}$ **c)** 0.665   **d)** 0.6   (1 mark)

3 Change $\frac{5}{8}$ into a decimal.

  a) 0.625   **b)** 0.425   **c)** 0.125   **d)** 0.725   (1 mark)

4 What is the **smallest** value in this list of numbers? 29%, 0.4, $\frac{3}{4}$, $\frac{1}{8}$

  a) 29%   **b)** 0.4   **c)** $\frac{3}{4}$ **d)** $\frac{1}{8}$ (1 mark)

5 What is the **largest** value in this list of numbers? $\frac{4}{5}$, 80%, $\frac{2}{3}$, 0.9

  a) $\frac{4}{5}$ **b)** 80%   **c)** $\frac{2}{3}$ **d)** 0.9   (1 mark)

Score   / 5

Short-answer questions

Answer all parts of each question.

1 The table shows equivalent fractions, decimals and percentages. Fill in the gaps.

Fraction	Decimal	Percentage
$\frac{2}{5}$		
		5%
	$0.\dot{3}$	
	0.04	
		25%
$\frac{1}{8}$		

(6 marks)

2 Decide whether these calculations give the same answer for this instruction:
increase £40 by 20%.

Jack says: Multiply 40 by 1.2   Hannah says: Work out 10%, double it and then add 40

Explain your reasoning.

_____

_____

(2 marks)

Score   / 8

Answer all parts of the questions. Show your workings (on a separate sheet of paper if necessary) and include the correct units in your answers.

1 Place these fractions in order of size, **smallest** first. $\frac{2}{3}, \frac{1}{10}, \frac{5}{8}, \frac{3}{5}, \frac{9}{10}$

(2 marks)

2 Write this list of seven numbers in order of size, **smallest** first.

25% $\frac{1}{3}$ 0.27 $\frac{2}{5}$ 0.571   72% $\frac{1}{8}$

(3 marks)

3 A sundial is being sold in two different garden centres. The cost of the sundial is £89.99 in both garden centres. Both garden centres have a promotion.

Gardens Are Us   Sundial 22% off

Rosebushes   Sundial $\frac{1}{4}$ off

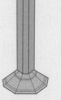

In which garden centre is the sundial **cheaper**? Explain your answer.

(2 marks)

4 Philippa is buying a new television. She sees three different advertisements for the same television set.

Ed's Electricals
TV normal price
£250
Sale 10% off

Sheila's Bargains
TV £185 plus
VAT at $17\frac{1}{2}$%

GITA's TV SHOP
Normal price
£290
Sale: $\frac{1}{5}$ off normal price

a) Philippa wants to buy her television from one of these shops, as cheaply as possible. Which shop should she choose and how much cheaper is it than the most expensive shop?

(5 marks)

b) The price of the television in a fourth shop is £235. This includes VAT at 17.5%. Work out the cost of the television before VAT was added.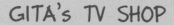

(3 marks)

Score   / 15

Number

For more information on this topic, see pages 10–13 and 16–20 of your Success Revision Guide.

Recurring decimals & surds

Multiple-choice questions

Choose just one answer, a, b, c or d. Circle your choice.

1 Which expression is equivalent to $\sqrt{12}$?

   a) $2\sqrt{6}$ **b)** $2\sqrt{3}$ **c)** $6\sqrt{2}$ **d)** $3\sqrt{2}$ **(1 mark)**

2 Which expression is equivalent to $\frac{1}{\sqrt{3}}$?

   a) $\frac{\sqrt{3}}{3}$ **b)** $\frac{\sqrt{3}}{9}$ **c)** $\frac{9}{\sqrt{3}}$ **d)** $\frac{3}{\sqrt{3}}$ **(1 mark)**

3 Which fraction is the same as $0.\dot{5}$?

   a) $\frac{1}{2}$ **b)** $\frac{5}{10}$ **c)** $\frac{5}{9}$ **d)** $\frac{5}{8}$ **(1 mark)**

4 Which fraction is equivalent to $0.\dot{6}\dot{3}...$?

   a) $\frac{63}{100}$ **b)** $\frac{6}{99}$ **c)** $\frac{636}{999}$ **d)** $\frac{7}{11}$ **(1 mark)**

5 Which fraction is equivalent to $0.2\dot{1}...$?

   a) $\frac{19}{90}$ **b)** $\frac{21}{99}$ **c)** $\frac{211}{999}$ **d)** $\frac{2}{9}$ **(1 mark)**

Score   / 5

Short-answer questions

Answer all parts of each question.

1 Express each of the following in the form $a\sqrt{b}$, where a and b are integers and b is as small as possible.

   a) $\sqrt{24}$ _____ **(1 mark)**

   b) $\sqrt{75}$ _____ **(1 mark)**

   c) $\sqrt{48} + \sqrt{12}$ _____ **(2 marks)**

   d) $\sqrt{80} + \sqrt{20}$ _____ **(2 marks)**

2 Rationalise the denominator $\frac{3}{\sqrt{2}}$

   _____ **(2 marks)**

3 Match each of the recurring decimals to its equivalent fraction.

   $0.\dot{7}$ $\frac{7}{9}$

   $0.\dot{2}\dot{4}$ $\frac{244}{333}$

   $0.\dot{7}3\dot{2}$ $\frac{13}{30}$

   $0.4\dot{3}$ $\frac{8}{33}$ **(4 marks)**

4 Find the fraction that is equivalent to $0.1\dot{2}\dot{5}$

   Express the fraction in its simplest form.

   _____ **(2 marks)**

Score   / 14

GCSE-style questions

Answer all parts of the questions. Show your workings (on a separate sheet of paper if necessary) and include the correct units in your answers.

1 a) Find the value of $\sqrt{3} \times \sqrt{27}$. _____ (1 mark)

b) $\sqrt{3} + \sqrt{27} = a\sqrt{3}$, where a is an integer. Find the value of a.

_____ (1 mark)

c) Find the value of $\dfrac{\sqrt{3} + \sqrt{12}}{\sqrt{75}}$ _____ (3 marks)

d) Rationalise the denominator $\dfrac{1}{\sqrt{3}}$ _____ (2 marks)

2 Work out $\dfrac{(5 + \sqrt{5})(2 - 2\sqrt{5})}{\sqrt{45}}$

Give your answer in its simplest form.

_____ (3 marks)

3 Simplify $(4 - \sqrt{3})^2$ _____ (2 marks)

4 Express $\dfrac{\sqrt{125} + \sqrt{50}}{\sqrt{5}}$ in the form $a + \sqrt{b}$. _____ (4 marks)

5 Work out $\dfrac{(2 - \sqrt{2})(4 + 3\sqrt{2})}{2}$

Give your answer in the form $a + b\sqrt{c}$.

_____ (3 marks)

6 Show that $\dfrac{2\sqrt{3} - 5}{\sqrt{3}}$ can be written as $2 - \dfrac{5\sqrt{3}}{3}$

_____ (3 marks)

7 Tick the boxes that are rational numbers.

$\sqrt{\dfrac{1}{49}}$	$\dfrac{\sqrt{18}}{\sqrt{2}}$	$\sqrt{12}$	$\sqrt{16} - \sqrt{4}$	$\sqrt{3.6}$

(3 marks)

8 a) Change the decimal $0.5\overset{..}{4}$ into a fraction in its simplest form.

_____ (2 marks)

b) Write the recurring decimal $0.02\overset{..}{6}$ as a fraction. _____ (2 marks)

9 Write down the recurring decimal $0.1\overset{..}{2}\overset{..}{3}$ in the form $\dfrac{a}{b}$ where a and b are integers.

_____ (2 marks)

10 Write down the recurring decimal $0.\overset{.}{7}$ as a fraction in its simplest form.

_____ (2 marks)

11 Prove that the recurring decimal $0.\overset{..}{4}\overset{..}{5}$ is $\dfrac{5}{11}$

_____ (3 marks)

Score _____ / 36

How well did you do?

| 0–17 | Try again | 18–28 | Getting there | 29–42 | Good work | 43–55 | Excellent! |

For more information on this topic, see page 21 of your Success Revision Guide.

Ratio

Multiple-choice questions

Choose just one answer, a, b, c or d. Circle your choice.

1 What is the ratio 6 : 18 written in its simplest form?

   a) 3 : 1   **b)** 3 : 9   **c)** 1 : 3   **d)** 9 : 3   **(1 mark)**

2 Write the ratio 200 : 500 in the form $1 : n$

   a) 1 : 50   **b)** 1 : 5   **c)** 1 : 25   **d)** 1 : 2.5   **(1 mark)**

3 If £140 is divided in the ratio 3 : 4, what is the size of the larger share?

   a) £45   **b)** £60   **c)** £80   **d)** £90   **(1 mark)**

4 A recipe for four people needs 800g of flour. How much flour is needed for six people?

   a) 12g   **b)** 120g   **c)** 12kg   **d)** 1200g   **(1 mark)**

5 If nine oranges cost £1.08, how much would 14 similar oranges cost? 🖩

   a) £1.50   **b)** £1.68   **c)** £1.20   **d)** £1.84   **(1 mark)**

Score   / 5

Short-answer questions

Answer all parts of each question.

1 Write down the ratio 10 : 15 in the form $1 : n$

                                          (1 mark)

2 It takes six people three days to dig and lay a cable. How long would it take four people? (All people work at the same rate.)

                            days   **(2 marks)**

3 a) Increase £4.10 in the ratio 2 : 5   **(1 mark)**

   b) Decrease 120g in the ratio 5 : 2   **(1 mark)**

4 Mrs London inherited £55 000. She divided the money between her children in the ratio 3 : 3 : 5. How much did the child with the largest share receive?

                                          (2 marks)

5 Seven bottles of lemonade have a total capacity of 1680ml. Work out the total capacity of five similar bottles. 🖩

                                  ml   **(1 mark)**

6 If £1 = 1.09 euros (€), change €726 into pounds. Give your answer to the nearest penny. 🖩

                                          (2 marks)

Score   / 10

GCSE-style questions

Answer all parts of the questions. Show your workings (on a separate sheet of paper if necessary) and include the correct units in your answers.

1 Vicky and Tracy share £14 400 in the ratio 4 : 5
How much does each of them receive?

Vicky: £ ....   Tracy: £ ....   **(3 marks)**

2 James uses these ingredients to make 12 buns:

> 50g butter, 40g sugar, 2 eggs, 45g flour, 15ml milk

James wants to make 18 similar buns. How much butter does James need?

.... g   **(1 mark)**

3 The table below shows the minimum ratio of staff to children in a particular crèche.

Age	Minimum adult : child ratio
Children under 2 years	1 : 3
Children aged 2 years	1 : 4
Children aged 3–5 years	1 : 8

On a Tuesday, the crèche has 17 children under 2 years, 14 children aged 2 years and 26 children aged 3–5 years. If each age group is in separate rooms, how many staff must the manager have working on a Tuesday?

....   **(3 marks)**

4 Tia went on holiday to Florida. The exchange rate was £1 = 1.65 American dollars ($).

a) Tia changed £750 into American dollars. How many dollars did Tia have? 🖩

$ ....   **(2 marks)**

b) When Tia returned from holiday she had $245 left. On the day she exchanged the dollars for pounds, the exchange rate had fallen to £1 = $1.49. Work out how much in pounds Tia got. Give your answer to the nearest penny. 🖩

£ ....   **(2 marks)**

5 7 metres of rope costs £5.46. Work out the cost of 13 metres of the same rope. 🖩

....   **(2 marks)**

6 Peas are sold in two different-sized tins. A small tin holds 142g and costs 24p. A large tin holds 300g and costs 49p. Which tin is the better value for money? You must show full working out to justify your answer. 🖩

....   **(4 marks)**

Score   / 17

Number

How well did you do?

| 0–8 | Try again | 9–18 | Getting there | 19–26 | Good work | 27–32 | Excellent! |

For more information on this topic, see pages 22–23 of your Success Revision Guide.

Indices

Multiple-choice questions

Choose just one answer, a, b, c or d. Circle your choice.

1 In index form, what is the value of $8^3 \times 8^{11}$?

    a) 8^{14} **b)** 8^{33} **c)** 64^{14} **d)** 64^{33} **(1 mark)**

2 In index form, what is the value of $7^{-12} \div 7^2$?

    a) 7^{10} **b)** 7^{-14} **c)** 7^{14} **d)** 7^{-10} **(1 mark)**

3 In index form, what is the value of $(4^2)^3$?

    a) 12^2 **b)** 4^5 **c)** 4^6 **d)** 16^6 **(1 mark)**

4 What is the value of 5^0?

    a) 5   **b)** 0   **c)** 25   **d)** 1   **(1 mark)**

5 What is the value of 5^{-2}?

    a) $\frac{1}{25}$ **b)** -5   **c)** 25   **d)** -25   **(1 mark)**

Score   / 5

Short-answer questions

Answer all parts of each question.

1 Evaluate these expressions.

    a) $25^{-\frac{1}{2}}$ _____   **b)** $49^{\frac{3}{2}}$ _____

    c) $\left(\frac{4}{5}\right)^{-2}$ _____   **d)** $81^{\frac{3}{4}}$ _____   **(4 marks)**

2 State whether each of these expressions is **true** or **false**.

    a) $a^4 \times a^5 = a^{20}$ _____   **(1 mark)**

    b) $2a^4 \times 3a^2 = 5a^8$ _____   **(1 mark)**

    c) $10a^6 \div 2a^4 = 5a^2$ _____   **(1 mark)**

    d) $20a^4b^2 \div 10a^5b = 20a^{-1}b$ _____   **(1 mark)**

    e) $(2a^3)^3 = 6a^9$ _____   **(1 mark)**

    f) $4^0 = 1$ _____   **(1 mark)**

3 Simplify the following expressions.

    a) $(5a)^0 =$ _____   **b)** $(2a^2)^4 =$ _____

    c) $12a^4 \div 16a^7 =$ _____   **d)** $(3a^2b^3)^3 =$ _____   **(4 marks)**

4 Write the following using negative indices.

    a) $\frac{4}{x^2} =$ _____   **b)** $\frac{a^2}{b^3} =$ _____   **c)** $\frac{3}{y^5} =$ _____   **(3 marks)**

Score   / 17

Answer all parts of the questions. Show your workings (on a separate sheet of paper if necessary) and include the correct units in your answers.

1 Hannah says that $3m^4 \times 5m^6$ is $8m^{10}$. Hannah is wrong. Explain why Hannah is wrong.

_____

_____ (1 mark)

2 Evaluate the following:

a) 3^0 _____ b) 9^{-2} _____ c) $3^4 \times 2^3$ _____

d) $64^{\frac{2}{3}}$ _____ e) $125^{-\frac{1}{3}}$ _____ (5 marks)

3 a) Evaluate the following:

   i) 8^0 _____ ii) 4^{-2} _____

   iii) $\left(\frac{4}{9}\right)^{-\frac{1}{2}}$ _____ (3 marks)

b) Write the following as a single power of 5.

   $\dfrac{5^7 \times 5^3}{(5^2)^3}$ _____ (2 marks)

4 Evaluate the following, giving your answers as fractions.

a) 5^{-3} _____ (1 mark)

b) $\left(\frac{2}{3}\right)^{-2}$ _____ (1 mark)

c) $(8)^{-\frac{2}{3}}$ _____ (1 mark)

5 Simplify the following, leaving your answer in the form 2^n.

a) $4^{-\frac{1}{2}}$ _____ (1 mark)

b) $\dfrac{2^7 \times 2^9}{2^{-4}}$ _____ (1 mark)

c) $(\sqrt{2})^5$ _____ (1 mark)

6 Simplify the following:

a) $p^3 \times p^4$ _____ (1 mark)

b) $\dfrac{n^3}{n^7}$ _____ (1 mark)

c) $\dfrac{a^3 \times a^4}{a}$ _____ (1 mark)

d) $\dfrac{12a^2b}{3a}$ _____ (1 mark)

7 Simplify the following expressions.

a) $(5x)^3$ _____ b) $(y^5)^4$ _____

c) $(3y)^{-3}$ _____ d) $(2xy^3)^5$ _____ (4 marks)

Score / 25

How well did you do?

| 0–14 Try again | 15–25 Getting there | 26–37 Good work | 38–47 Excellent! |

For more information on this topic, see pages 24–25 of your Success Revision Guide.

Standard index form

Multiple-choice questions

Choose just one answer, a, b, c or d. Circle your choice.

1 What is 42 710 written in standard form?

   a) 42.71×10^3 **b)** 4.271×10^4 **c)** 4271.0×10 **d)** 427.1×10^2 (1 mark)

2 What is 6.4×10^{-3} written as an ordinary number?

   a) 6400   **b)** 0.0064   **c)** 64   **d)** 0.064   (1 mark)

3 What is 2.7×10^4 written as an ordinary number?

   a) 27 000   **b)** 0.27   **c)** 270   **d)** 0.000 27   (1 mark)

4 What is $(4 \times 10^9) \times (2 \times 10^6)$ worked out and written in standard form?

   a) 8×10^{54} **b)** 8×10^{15} **c)** 8×10^3 **d)** 6×10^{15} (1 mark)

5 What is $(3 \times 10^4)^2$ worked out and written in standard form?

   a) 9×10^6 **b)** 9×10^8 **c)** 9×10^9 **d)** 3×10^8 (1 mark)

Score   / 5

Short-answer questions

Answer all parts of each question.

1 State whether each of the statements is **true** or **false**.

   a) 4710 is 4.71×10^3 written in standard form. _____ (1 mark)

   b) 249 000 is 24.9×10^4 written in standard form. _____ (1 mark)

   c) 0.047 is 47×10^{-3} written in standard form. _____ (1 mark)

   d) 0.000 009 6 is 9.6×10^{-7} written in standard form. _____ (1 mark)

2 Work out the following calculations. Give your answers in standard form.

   a) $(3 \times 10^6) \times (2 \times 10^3)$ _____ (1 mark)

   b) $(7 \times 10^{-3}) \times (2 \times 10^6)$ _____ (1 mark)

   c) $(9 \times 10^{12}) \div (3 \times 10^{-4})$ _____ (1 mark)

3 Work out the following calculations. Give your answers in standard form. 🖩

   a) $(2.1 \times 10^7) \times (3.9 \times 10^{-4})$ _____ (1 mark)

   b) $(6.3 \times 10^{-4}) \times (1.2 \times 10^6)$ _____ (1 mark)

   c) $(1.2 \times 10^{-9}) \div (2 \times 10^{-3})$ _____ (1 mark)

4 The mass of an atom is 2×10^{-23} grams. What is the total mass of 9×10^{15} of these atoms? Give your answer in standard form. 🖩

_____ (3 marks)

Score   / 13

Answer all parts of the questions. Show your workings (on a separate sheet of paper if necessary) and include the correct units in your answers.

1 a) i) Write the number 2.07×10^5 as an ordinary number.

(1 mark)

ii) Write the number 0.000 046 in standard form.

(1 mark)

b) Work out 7×10^4 multiplied by 5×10^7.
Give your answer in standard form.

(2 marks)

2 A 1 ounce measure of grass seeds contains approximately 2.7×10^4 seeds. Given that 1 ounce is equal to 28.3g, work out how many grass seeds would be in a 1kg measure of seeds. Give your answer in standard form, correct to 3 significant figures. 🖩

(3 marks)

3 If $a = 3.2 \times 10^4$ and $b = 2 \times 10^{-3}$, calculate the answer to $\dfrac{b^2}{a + b}$ giving your answer in standard form, correct to 3 significant figures. 🖩

(2 marks)

4 The mass of Saturn is 5.7×10^{26} tonnes. The mass of the Earth is 6.1×10^{21} tonnes. How many times heavier is Saturn than the Earth? Give your answer in standard form, correct to 1 decimal place. 🖩

(3 marks)

5 a) Five investors buy a warehouse for £4.3 million. They each contribute the same amount. How much does each investor pay? Give your answer in standard form. 🖩

£

(2 marks)

b) After converting the warehouse into luxury apartments, the investors make a profit of £3.1 million. How much profit does each investor make? Give your answer in standard form. 🖩

£

(2 marks)

6 A water molecule has a mass of 3×10^{-26}kg. A container holds 2.4×10^{26} molecules of water. Work out the mass of the water in the container. Give your answer in grams. 🖩

g

(3 marks)

Score   / 19

Number

How well did you do?

| 0–9 | Try again | 10–18 | Getting there | 19–28 | Good work | 29–37 | Excellent! |

For more information on this topic, see pages 26–27 of your Success Revision Guide.

Upper & lower bounds of measurement

Multiple-choice questions

Choose just one answer, a, b, c or d. Circle your choice.

1 The length of an object is 5.6cm, correct to the nearest millimetre. What is the lower bound of the length of the object?

    a) 5.56cm   **b)** 5.55cm   **c)** 5.64cm   **d)** 5.65cm   (1 mark)

2 The mass of an object is 2.23 grams, correct to 2 decimal places. What is the upper bound of the mass of the object?

    a) 2.225g   **b)** 2.234g   **c)** 2.235g   **d)** 2.32g   (1 mark)

3 A hall can hold 40 people to the nearest 10. What is the upper bound for the number of people in the hall?

    a) 45   **b)** 35   **c)** 44   **d)** 36   (1 mark)

4 A square has a length of 3cm to the nearest centimetre. What is the lower bound for the perimeter of the square? 🖩

    a) 12cm   **b)** 10cm   **c)** 10.4cm   **d)** 14cm   (1 mark)

5 Using the information given in question 4, what is the upper bound for the area of the square? 🖩

    a) $6.25cm^2$ **b)** $9cm^2$ **c)** $12.5cm^2$ **d)** $12.25cm^2$ (1 mark)

Score   / 5

Short-answer questions

Answer all parts of each question.

1 A book has a mass of 112 grams, correct to the nearest gram.

    a) Write down the lowest possible mass of the book. _____ g   (1 mark)

    b) Write down the highest possible mass of the book. _____ g   (1 mark)

2 $a = \dfrac{(3.4)^2 \times 12.68}{2.4}$

3.4 and 2.4 are correct to 1 decimal place. 12.68 is correct to 2 decimal places. Which of the following calculations gives the lower bound for a and the upper bound for a? (Write down the letters.)

  A $\dfrac{(3.45)^2 \times 12.685}{2.35}$ **B** $\dfrac{(3.35)^2 \times 12.675}{2.35}$ **C** $\dfrac{(3.45)^2 \times 12.685}{2.45}$

  D $\dfrac{(3.45)^2 \times 12.675}{2.35}$ **E** $\dfrac{(3.35)^2 \times 12.675}{2.45}$

Lower bound _____   Upper bound _____   (2 marks)

3 To the nearest centimetre, $a = 3$cm, $b = 5$cm. Calculate the lower bound for ab. 🖩

_____ cm^2 (2 marks)

Score   / 6

24

Answer all parts of the questions. Show your workings (on a separate sheet of paper if necessary) and include the correct units in your answers.

1 $p = 3.1$cm and $q = 4.7$cm, correct to 1 decimal place.

  a) Calculate the upper bound for the value of $p + q$.

  _____ (2 marks)

  b) Calculate the lower bound for the value of $\frac{p}{q}$

  Give your answer correct to 3 significant figures.

  _____

  _____ (3 marks)

2 A ball is thrown vertically upwards with a speed V metres per second. The height, H metres, to which it rises is given by:

  $$H = \frac{V^2}{2g}$$ where g m/s^2 is the acceleration due to gravity.

  $V = 32.6$ correct to 3 significant figures. $g = 9.8$ correct to 2 significant figures.

  Calculate the difference between the lower and upper bound of H.
  Give your answer correct to 3 significant figures.

  _____

  _____ m (5 marks)

3 Jaydn drove for 146 miles, correct to the nearest mile. He used 15.6 litres of petrol to the nearest tenth of a litre.

  $$\text{Petrol consumption} = \frac{\text{number of miles travelled}}{\text{number of litres of petrol used}}$$

  Jaydn claims that his petrol consumption is less than 9.3 miles per litre. Explain whether his claim is correct. You must show full working out to justify your answer.

  _____

  _____ (3 marks)

4 The volume of a cube is given as 62.7cm^3, correct to 1 decimal place. Find the upper and lower bounds for the length of an edge of this cube, to 5 significant figures.

  Lower bound = _____ Upper bound = _____ (4 marks)

5 The weight of a bag of flour is given as 2kg, but it is found to have an actual weight of 2.21kg. Calculate the percentage error.

  _____ (2 marks)

Score   / 19

Number

How well did you do?

| 0–6 | Try again | 7–13 | Getting there | 14–22 | Good work | 23–30 | Excellent! |

For more information on this topic, see pages 28–29 and 79 of your Success Revision Guide.

Algebra & formulae

Multiple-choice questions

Choose just one answer, a, b, c or d. Circle your choice.

1 What is the expression $7a - 4b + 6a - 3b$ when it is fully simplified?

   a) $7b - a$ **b)** $13a + 7b$ **c)** $a - 7b$ **d)** $13a - 7b$ (1 mark)

2 What is $(n - 3)^2$ when it is multiplied out and simplified?

   a) $n^2 + 9$ **b)** $n^2 + 6n - 9$ **c)** $n^2 - 6n - 9$ **d)** $n^2 - 6n + 9$ (1 mark)

3 Factorising $n^2 + 7n - 8$ gives which of the following?

   a) $(n - 2)(n - 6)$ **b)** $(n - 2)(n + 4)$ **c)** $(n - 1)(n + 8)$ **d)** $(n + 1)(n - 8)$ (1 mark)

4 If $m = \sqrt{\dfrac{r^2 p}{4}}$ and $r = 3$ and $p = 6$, what is the value of m to 1 decimal place? 🔲

   a) 13.5   **b)** 182.3   **c)** 3.7   **d)** 3   (1 mark)

5 $P = a^2 + b$. Rearrange this formula to make a the subject.

   a) $a = \pm\sqrt{(P - b)}$ **b)** $a = \pm\sqrt{(P + b)}$ **c)** $a = \dfrac{P - b}{2}$ **d)** $a = \dfrac{P + b}{2}$ (1 mark)

Score   / 5

Short-answer questions

Answer all parts of each question.

1 John buys b books costing £6 each and p magazines costing 67 pence each. Write down a formula for the total cost (T) of the books and magazines.

   $T =$ _____   (2 marks)

2 Factorise the following expressions.

   a) $10n + 15$ _____   **b)** $24 - 36n$ _____

   c) $n^2 + 6n + 5$ _____   **d)** $n^2 - 64$ _____

   e) $n^2 - 3n - 4$ _____   (5 marks)

3 $a = \dfrac{b^2 + 2c}{4}$

   a) Calculate a if $b = 2$ and $c = 6$ _____   (1 mark)

   b) Calculate a if $b = 3$ and $c = 5.5$ _____   (1 mark)

   c) Calculate b if $a = 25$ and $c = 18$ _____   (1 mark)

4 Rearrange each of the formulae below to make b the subject.

   a) $p = 3b - 4$ _____   (1 mark)

   b) $y = \dfrac{b^2 - 6}{4}$ _____   (1 mark)

   c) $5(n + b) = 2b + 2$ _____   (1 mark)

Score   / 13

Answer all parts of the questions. Show your workings (on a separate sheet of paper if necessary) and include the correct units in your answers.

1 **a)** Expand and simplify $3(2x + 1) - 2(x - 2)$.

(2 marks)

b) **i)** Factorise $6a + 12$.

(1 mark)

ii) Factorise completely $10a^2 - 15ab$.

(2 marks)

c) **i)** Factorise $n^2 + 5n + 6$.

(2 marks)

ii) Hence simplify fully $\dfrac{2(n + 3)}{n^2 + 5n + 6}$

(2 marks)

d) Factorise fully $(x + y)^2 - 2(x + y)$.

(2 marks)

2 Show that $(n - 1)^2 + n + (n - 1)$ simplifies to n^2.

(3 marks)

3 Simplify fully $\dfrac{x^2 - 8x}{x^2 - 9x + 8}$

(3 marks)

4 Prove that the sum of two consecutive whole numbers is always odd.

(3 marks)

5 A person's body mass index (BMI), b, is calculated using the formula:

$$b = \frac{m}{h^2}$$

where m is the person's mass in kilograms and h is their height in metres.

A person is classed as overweight if their BMI is greater than 25. Peter has a height of 184cm and a mass of 89.5kg. Would Peter be classed as overweight? You must show working to justify your answer. 🖩

(3 marks)

Score   / 23

Algebra

How well did you do?

| 0–13 | Try again | 14–22 | Getting there | 23–33 | Good work | 34–41 | Excellent! |

For more information on this topic, see pages 32–35 and 42–43 of your Success Revision Guide.

Equations

Multiple-choice questions

Choose just one answer, a, b, c or d. Circle your choice.

1 Solve the equation $4n - 2 = 10$.

    a) $n = 4$ **b)** $n = 2$ **c)** $n = 3$ **d)** $n = 3.5$ (1 mark)

2 Solve the equation $4(x + 3) = 16$.

    a) $x = 9$ **.b)** $x = 7$ **c)** $x = 4$ **d)** $x = 1$ (1 mark)

3 Solve the equation $4(n + 2) = 8(n - 3)$.

    a) $n = 16$ **b)** $n = 8$ **c)** $n = 4$ **d)** $n = 12$ (1 mark)

4 Solve the equation $10 - 6n = 4n - 5$.

    a) $n = 2$ **b)** $n = -2$ **c)** $n = 1.5$ **d)** $n = -1.5$ (1 mark)

5 Solve the equation $2x^2 - x - 3 = 0$.

    a) $x = \frac{3}{2}, x = 1$ **b)** $x = \frac{2}{3}, x = -1$ **c)** $x = \frac{3}{2}, x = -1$ **d)** $x = \frac{2}{3}, x = 1$ (1 mark)

Score   / 5

Short-answer questions

Answer all parts of each question.

1 Solve the following equations.

    a) $5n = 25$ **b)** $\frac{n}{3} = 12$

    c) $2n - 4 = 10$ **d)** $3 - 2n = 14$

    e) $\frac{n}{5} + 2 = 7$ **f)** $4 - \frac{n}{2} = 2$ (6 marks)

2 Solve the following equations.

    a) $12n + 5 = 3n + 32$ **b)** $5n - 4 = 3n + 6$

    c) $5(n + 1) = 25$ **d)** $4(n - 2) = 3(n + 2)$ (4 marks)

3 Solve the following equations.

    a) $n^2 - 4n = 0$ **b)** $n^2 + 6n + 5 = 0$

    c) $n^2 - 5n + 6 = 0$ **d)** $n^2 - 3n - 28 = 0$ (4 marks)

4 The angles in a triangle add up to 180°. Form an equation in terms of n and solve it.

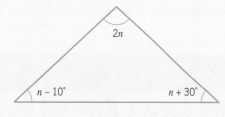

$n =$ (2 marks)

Score   / 16

GCSE-style questions

Answer all parts of the questions. Show your workings (on a separate sheet of paper if necessary) and include the correct units in your answers.

1 Solve these equations.

a) $5m - 3 = 12$ $m =$ _____   (2 marks)

b) $8p + 3 = 9 - 2p$ $p =$ _____   (2 marks)

c) $5(x - 1) = 3x + 7$ $x =$ _____   (2 marks)

d) $\frac{w}{2} + \frac{(3w + 2)}{3} = \frac{1}{3}$ $w =$ _____   (2 marks)

2 a) Solve $6p + 3 = 2p + 11$.

_____

(2 marks)

b) Solve $5y + 2 = 2(y - 4)$.

_____

(2 marks)

3 The width of a rectangle is y centimetres. The length of the rectangle is 2 centimetres more than the width. The perimeter of the rectangle is 64 centimetres. Work out the length of the rectangle.

_____

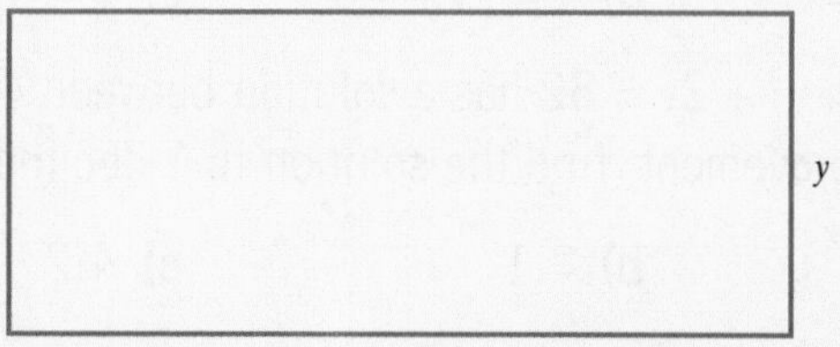

(4 marks)

4 Solve the equation $x^2 - 4x + 3 = 0$.

$x =$ _____ and $x =$ _____   (3 marks)

5 The diagram shows an irregular pentagon.

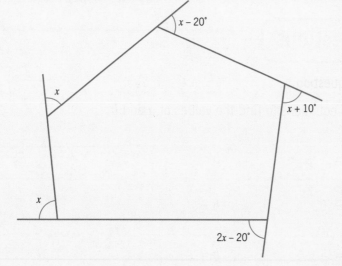

Work out the size of the largest exterior angle.

_____

(3 marks)

Score   / 22

How well did you do?

| 0–14 | Try again | 15–22 | Getting there | 23–35 | Good work | 36–43 | Excellent! |

For more information on this topic, see pages 36–39 and 59 of your Success Revision Guide.

Equations & inequalities

Multiple-choice questions

Choose just one answer, a, b, c or d. Circle your choice.

1 Solve these simultaneous equations to find the values of a and b.

$a + b = 10$

$2a - b = 2$

   a) $a = 4, b = 6$ **b)** $a = 4, b = -2$ **c)** $a = 5, b = 5$ **d)** $a = 3, b = 7$ (1 mark)

2 Solve these simultaneous equations to find the values of x and y.

$3x - y = 7$

$2x + y = 3$

   a) $x = 3, y = 2$ **b)** $x = 2, y = 1$ **c)** $x = -3, y = 2$ **d)** $x = 2, y = -1$ (1 mark)

3 The equation $y^3 + 2y = 82$ has a solution between 4 and 5. By using a method of trial and improvement, find the solution to 1 decimal place. 🔢

   a) 3.9   **b)** 4.1   **c)** 4.2   **d)** 4.3   (1 mark)

4 Solve the inequality $3x + 1 < 19$.

   a) $x < 3$ **b)** $x < 7$ **c)** $x < 5$ **d)** $x < 6$ (1 mark)

5 Solve the inequality $2x - 7 < 9$.

   a) $x < 9$ **b)** $x < 10$ **c)** $x < 8$ **d)** $x < 6.5$ (1 mark)

Score   / 5

Short-answer questions

Answer all parts of each question.

1 Solve these simultaneous equations to find the values of a and b.

   a) $2a + b = 8$

       $3a - b = 2$ $a =$ .... $b =$ ....   (2 marks)

   b) $5a + b = 24$

       $2a + 2b = 24$ $a =$ .... $b =$ ....   (2 marks)

   c) $4a + 3b = 6$

       $2a - 3b = 12$ $a =$ .... $b =$ ....   (2 marks)

2 The solution to the equation $t^2 - 2t = 20$ lies between 5 and 6. Find this solution by using a method of trial and improvement. Give your answer to 1 decimal place. 🔢

    ....   (2 marks)

3 Solve the following inequalities.

   a) $5x + 2 < 12$ ....   **b)** $\frac{x}{3} + 1 \geqslant 3$ ....

   c) $3 \leqslant 2x + 1 \leqslant 9$ ....   **d)** $3 \leqslant 3x + 2 \leqslant 8$ ....   (4 marks)

Score   / 12

Answer all parts of the questions. Show your workings (on a separate sheet of paper if necessary) and include the correct units in your answers.

1 n is an integer.

   a) Write down the integer values of n that satisfy the inequality $-4 < n \leqslant 2$.

(2 marks)

   b) Solve the inequality $5p - 2 \leqslant 8$. (2 marks)

2 Use the method of trial and improvement to solve the equation $x^3 + 3x = 28$. Give your answer correct to 1 decimal place. You must show all your working. 📱

(4 marks)

3 Solve these simultaneous equations.

   $3x - 2y = -12$ $2x + 6y = 3$ $x =$ _____ $y =$ _____   (4 marks)

4 The Gray family, Mr and Mrs Gray and their three children, pay £45 to get into a zoo. The Khan family, Mr and Mrs Khan, their grown-up son and four children, pay £63.75 to get into the zoo. How much are adult and child tickets for the zoo?

(4 marks)

5 The region R satisfies the inequalities:

   $x \geqslant 1$ $y \geqslant 2$ $x + y \leqslant 8$

   On the grid below, draw straight lines and use shading to show the region R.

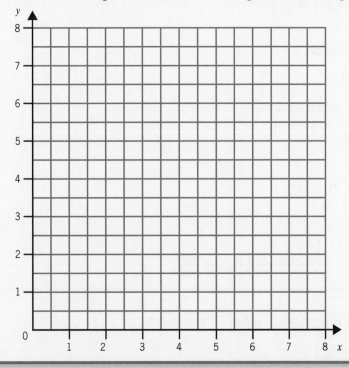

(3 marks)

Score   / 19

How well did you do?

| 0–9 | Try again | 10–18 | Getting there | 19–27 | Good work | 28–36 | Excellent! |

For more information on this topic, see pages 38–39 and 41 of your Success Revision Guide.

Advanced algebra & equations

Multiple-choice questions

Choose just one answer, a, b, c or d. Circle your choice.

1 The expression $x^2 + 4x + 7$ is written in the form $(x + a)^2 + b$.
What are the values of a and b?

  a) $a = 3, b = 6$ **b)** $a = 4, b = -3$ **c)** $a = 2, b = 3$ **d)** $a = 4, b = 2$ **(1 mark)**

2 The expression $x^2 - 2x + 3$ is written in the form $(x + a)^2 + b$.
What are the values of a and b?

  a) $a = 1, b = 2$ **b)** $a = -1, b = -2$ **c)** $a = -1, b = 2$ **d)** $a = 1, b = -2$ **(1 mark)**

3 What are the solutions of the quadratic equation $x^2 - 4 = 0$?

  a) $x = 2, x = 2$ **b)** $x = -2, x = -2$ **c)** $x = 0, x = 4$ **d)** $x = 2, x = -2$ **(1 mark)**

4 What are the solutions of the quadratic equation $6x^2 + 2x = 8$?

  a) $x = 1, x = \frac{3}{4}$ **b)** $x = 1, x = -\frac{4}{3}$ **c)** $x = -1, x = \frac{4}{3}$ **d)** $x = -1, x = -\frac{3}{4}$ **(1 mark)**

5 What are the solutions of the quadratic equation $2x^2 + 5x + 2 = 0$?

  a) $x = -\frac{1}{2}, x = -2$ **b)** $x = \frac{1}{2}, x = -2$ **c)** $x = -\frac{1}{2}, x = 2$ **d)** $x = 2, x = -2$ **(1 mark)**

Score   / 5

Short-answer questions

Answer all parts of each question.

1 a) Factorise $x^2 + 11x + 30$. _____ **(2 marks)**

  b) Write the following as a single fraction in its simplest form.

    $\dfrac{4}{(x + 6)} + \dfrac{4}{(x^2 + 11x + 30)}$ _____ **(4 marks)**

2 $(x + 4)(x - 3) = 2$

  a) Show that $x^2 + x - 14 = 0$.

  _____ **(2 marks)**

  b) Solve the equation $x^2 + x - 14 = 0$.
    Give your answers correct to 3 significant figures. 🖩

  _____ **(3 marks)**

3 The formula $a = \dfrac{3(b + c)}{bc}$ is rearranged to make c the subject.

  Greg says the answer is $c = \dfrac{3b}{ab - 3}$

  Decide whether Greg is right. You must justify your answer.

  _____

  _____ **(3 marks)**

Score   / 14

Answer all parts of the questions. Show your workings (on a separate sheet of paper if necessary) and include the correct units in your answers.

1 The expression $x^2 + 6x + 3$ can be written in the form $(x + a)^2 + b$ for all values of x.

a) Find a and b.

$a =$ _____

$b =$ _____ (3 marks)

b) The expression $x^2 + 6x + 3$ has a minimum value. Using your answer to part a), find this minimum value.

_____

_____ (1 mark)

2 Make b the subject of the formula $a = \dfrac{8b + 5}{4 - 3b}$

_____

_____ (4 marks)

3 The diagram shows a right-angled triangle with base $(x - 3)$ and height $(x + 4)$. All measurements are in centimetres. The area of the triangle is 12 square centimetres.

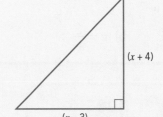

a) Show that $x^2 + x - 36 = 0$.

_____

_____ (3 marks)

b) Find the length of the base of the triangle. Give your answer correct to 2 decimal places. 🖩

_____

_____ cm (4 marks)

4 Make a the subject of the formula $P = 4a + \pi a + 3b$.

_____

_____ (3 marks)

5 Solve the equation $2x^2 - 7x = 6$. Give your solutions correct to 3 significant figures. 🖩

_____ (3 marks)

Score   / 21

How well did you do?

| 0–7 | Try again | 8–18 | Getting there | 19–30 | Good work | 31–40 | Excellent! |

For more information on this topic, see pages 32–37 and 42–44 of your Success Revision Guide.

Direct & inverse proportion

Multiple-choice questions

Choose just one answer, a, b, c or d. Circle your choice.

1 If a is directly proportional to b and $a = 10$ when $b = 5$, what is the formula that connects a and b?

a) $a = 5b$ **b)** $a = 10b$ **c)** $a = \frac{1}{2}b$ **d)** $a = 2b$ (1 mark)

2 If y is directly proportional to x and $y = 12$ when $x = 4$, what is the formula that connects x and y?

a) $y = 3x$ **b)** $x = 3y$ **c)** $y = 12x$ **d)** $y = \frac{1}{3x}$ (1 mark)

3 If d is inversely proportional to c, so that $d = \frac{k}{c}$, what is the value of k when $d = 6$ and $c = 3$?

a) 12   **b)** 18   **c)** 2   **d)** 9   (1 mark)

4 If v is inversely proportional to w^2 and $v = 3$ when $w = 2$, what is the formula that connects v and w^2?

a) $v = \frac{18}{w^2}$ **b)** $v = \frac{2}{w^2}$ **c)** $v = \frac{12}{w^2}$ **d)** $v = \frac{3}{2w^2}$ (1 mark)

Score   / 4

Short-answer questions

Answer all parts of each question.

1 The variables x and y are related so that y is directly proportional to the square of x. Complete this table for values of x and y.

x	2	4	....	....
y	12	....	27	75

(3 marks)

2 z is inversely proportional to the square of v.

a) Express z in terms of v and a constant of proportionality k.

_____

(2 marks)

b) If $z = 10$ when $v = 5$, calculate... 🖩

    i) the value of z when $v = 2$ .... (2 marks)

    ii) the value of v when $z = 1000$ .... (2 marks)

3 m is inversely proportional to t. $m = 20$ when $t = 8$. Calculate the value of m when $t = 32$. 🖩

_____

_____

(2 marks)

Score   / 11

GCSE-style questions

Answer all parts of the questions. Show your workings (on a separate sheet of paper if necessary) and include the correct units in your answers.

1 D is directly proportional to the square of y. When $D = 16$, $y = 2$. Calculate the value of D when $y = 9$.

_____

(3 marks)

2 The extension (E) of a spring is directly proportional to the force (F) pulling the spring. The extension is 6cm when a force of 15N is pulling it. Calculate the extension when the force is 80N. 🖩

_____

_____ cm   (4 marks)

3 The volume (V) of a toy is proportional to the cube of its height (h). When the toy's volume is 60cm³, the height is 2cm. Find the volume of a similar toy whose height is 5cm. 🖩

_____

_____ cm³   (4 marks)

4 I is inversely proportional to the square of d. When $d = 2$, $I = 50$.

   a) Calculate, to 1 decimal place, the value of I when d is 3.5 🖩

_____

(3 marks)

   b) Calculate the value of d when I is 12.5 🖩

_____

_____

(3 marks)

5 The frequency (f) of sound is inversely proportional to the wavelength (w). A sound with a frequency of 45 hertz has a wavelength of 16.2 metres. Calculate the wavelength when a sound has a frequency of 24 hertz. 🖩

_____

_____ m   (4 marks)

6 c is inversely proportional to b and $b = 10$ when $c = 4$.
Daisy says that the formula connecting c and b is given by $c = \dfrac{40}{b}$

Decide whether Daisy is correct, giving a reason for your answer.

_____

_____

(2 marks)

Score   / 23

How well did you do?

| 0–7 | Try again | 8–16 | Getting there | 17–27 | Good work | 28–38 | Excellent! |

For more information on this topic, see page 45 of your Success Revision Guide.

Straight-line graphs

Multiple-choice questions

Choose just one answer, a, b, c or d. Circle your choice.

1 Which pair of coordinates lies on the line $x = 2$?

   a) (1, 3)   **b)** (2, 3)   **c)** (3, 2)   **d)** (0, 2)   (1 mark)

2 Which pair of coordinates lies on the line $y = -3$?

   a) (-3, 5)   **b)** (5, -2)   **c)** (-2, 5)   **d)** (5, -3)   (1 mark)

3 What is the gradient of the line $y = 2 - 5x$?

   a) -2   **b)** -5   **c)** 2   **d)** 5   (1 mark)

4 These graphs have been drawn: $y = 3x - 1$, $y = 5 - 2x$, $y = 6x + 1$, $y = 2x - 3$
   Which graph is the **steepest**?

   a) $y = 3x - 1$ **b)** $y = 5 - 2x$ **c)** $y = 6x + 1$ **d)** $y = 2x - 3$ (1 mark)

5 At which point does the graph $y = 3x - 4$ intercept the y-axis?

   a) (0, -4)   **b)** (0, 3)   **c)** (-4, 0)   **d)** (3, 0)   (1 mark)

Score   / 5

Short-answer questions

Answer all parts of each question.

1 a) On the grid, draw the graph of $y = 6 - x$.
   Join your points with a straight line.

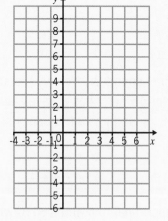

(2 marks)

b) A second line goes through the coordinates
   (1, 5), (-2, -4) and (2, 8).

   i) Draw this line on the grid.   (1 mark)

   ii) Write down the equation of the line you have just drawn.

   _____   (2 marks)

c) What are the coordinates of the point where the two lines intercept?

   _____   (1 mark)

2 The equations of five straight lines are: $y = 2x - 4$, $y = 3 - 2x$, $y = 4 - 2x$, $y = 5x - 4$, $y = 3x - 5$. Two of the lines are parallel. Write down the equations of these two lines.

_____ and _____   (2 marks)

Score   / 8

GCSE-style questions

Answer all parts of the questions. Show your workings (on a separate sheet of paper if necessary) and include the correct units in your answers.

1 Three of the following points lie on the line $y = 3x - 4$.

(-1, -5)	(-2, -10)	(2, 3)	(1, -1)	(5, 10)	(0, -4)

Tick the boxes under the coordinates of the correct points.   (1 mark)

2 The line with equation $3y + 2x = 12$ has been drawn on the grid.

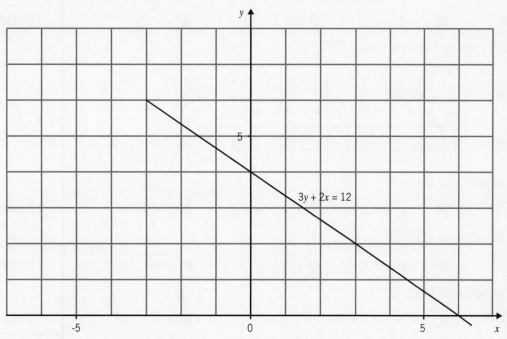

$3y + 2x = 12$

a) On the grid above, draw the graph with the equation $3y - x = 3$.   (2 marks)

b) Write down the coordinates of the point of intersection of the two straight-line graphs $3y + 2x = 12$ and $3y - x = 3$.

(................., ...)   (1 mark)

c) Write down the gradient of the line $3y + 2x = 12$.

....   (2 marks)

d) Write down the equation of the line that is parallel to $3y + 2x = 12$ and passes through the point with coordinates (0, 2).

....   (1 mark)

e) Write down the gradient of a line that is perpendicular to the line $3y + 2x = 12$.

....   (1 mark)

Score   / 8

How well did you do?

| 0–4 | Try again | 5–9 | Getting there | 10–14 | Good work | 15–21 | Excellent! |

For more information on this topic, see page 46–47 of your Success Revision Guide.

Curved graphs

Multiple-choice questions

Choose just one answer, a, b, c or d. Circle your choice.

1 Which pair of coordinates lies on the graph $y = x^2 - 2$?

　a) $(1, 1)$　　　　**b)** $(4, 14)$　　　　**c)** $(2, 4)$　　　　**d)** $(0, 2)$　　(1 mark)

2 On which of these curves do the coordinates $(2, 5)$ lie?

　a) $y = x^2 - 4$　　**b)** $y = 2x^2 + 3$　　**c)** $y = x^2 - 6$　　**d)** $y = 2x^2 - 3$　　(1 mark)

Questions 3–5 refer to these graphs:

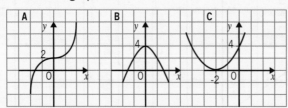

3 What is the equation of graph A?

　a) $y = 5 - 2x^2$　　**b)** $y = x^2 + 4x + 4$　**c)** $y = x^3 + 2$　　**d)** $y = 4 - x^2$　　(1 mark)

4 What is the equation of graph B?

　a) $y = 5 - 2x^2$　　**b)** $y = x^2 + 4x + 4$　**c)** $y = x^3 + 2$　　**d)** $y = 4 - x^2$　　(1 mark)

5 What is the equation of graph C?

　a) $y = 5 - 2x^2$　　**b)** $y = x^2 + 4x + 4$　**c)** $y = x^3 + 2$　　**d)** $y = 4 - x^2$　　(1 mark)

Score　/ 5

Short-answer questions

Answer all parts of each question.

1 **a)** Complete the table of values for $y = x^2 - 2x - 2$.

x	-2	-1	0	1	2	3
$y = x^2 - 2x - 2$			-2			1

(2 marks)

b) On the grid below, draw the graph of $y = x^2 - 2x - 2$.　　(3 marks)

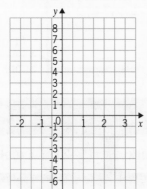

c) Use your graph to write down an estimate for...

　i) the minimum value of y

　　$y =$ _____　　(1 mark)

　ii) the solutions of the equation $x^2 - 2x - 2 = 0$

　　$x =$ _____ and $x =$ _____　　(2 marks)

Score　/ 8

GCSE-style questions

Answer all parts of the questions. Show your workings (on a separate sheet of paper if necessary) and include the correct units in your answers.

1 **a)** Complete the table of values for the graph $y = x^3 - 4$. 📱

x	-2	-1	0	1	2	3
$y = x^3 - 4$	....	-5	....	....	....	23

(2 marks)

b) On the grid, draw the graph of $y = x^3 - 4$ for values of x between -2 and 3.

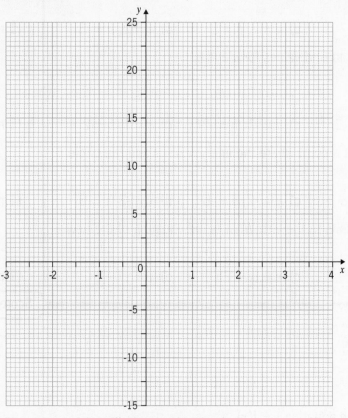

(2 marks)

c) Use your graph to find an estimate of...

i) the solution of the equation $x^3 - 4 = 0$

$x = $ .... **(1 mark)**

ii) the solution of the equation $x^3 - 4 = 10$

$x = $ .... **(2 marks)**

iii) the solution of the equation $x^3 - 4 = 2$

$x = $ .... **(2 marks)**

iv) the solution of the equation $x^3 - 4 = -7$

$x = $ .... **(2 marks)**

Score   / 11

How well did you do?

| 0–5 | Try again | 6–11 | Getting there | 12–17 | Good work | 18–24 | Excellent! |

For more information on this topic, see pages 48–49 of your Success Revision Guide.

Advanced graphs

Multiple-choice questions

Choose just one answer, a, b, c or d. Circle your choice.

1 Solve these simultaneous equations to find values for a and b.
$$a^2 + b^2 = 13$$
$$2a + b = 7$$

   a) $a = -2, b = 3$ **b)** $a = 3, b = 2$ **c)** $a = 2, b = 3$ **d)** $a = 2, b = -3$ (1 mark)

2 Solve these simultaneous equations to find values for a and b.
$$a^2 - b = 3$$
$$3a + b = 1$$

   a) $a = 1, b = -2$ **b)** $a = -1, b = 2$ **c)** $a = -1, b = -2$ **d)** $a = 1, b = 2$ (1 mark)

3 What are the possible coordinates of a point where the line $y = 4 - x$ and the circle $x^2 + y^2 = 40$ meet?

   a) $x = 2, y = -6$ **b)** $x = 2, y = 6$ **c)** $x = -2, y = -6$ **d)** $x = -2, y = 6$ (1 mark)

4 The graph $y = x^2$ is translated two units to the left. What is the equation of the new curve?

   a) $y = (x - 2)^2$ **b)** $y = x^2 + 2$ **c)** $y = (x + 2)^2$ **d)** $y = x^2 - 2$ (1 mark)

Score   / 4

Short-answer questions

Answer all parts of each question.

1 This is a sketch of the curve with the equation $y = f(x)$.
The maximum point of the curve is A (2, 7).
Write down the coordinates of the maximum
point of each of the following curves.

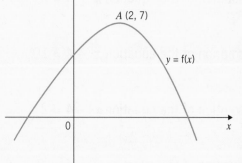

   a) $y = f(x) - 3$ (................, ...)   (1 mark)

   b) $y = f(x + 1)$ (................, ...)   (1 mark)

   c) $y = f(x - 4)$ (................, ...)   (1 mark)

   d) $y = f(-x)$ (................, ...)   (1 mark)

   e) $y = f(2x)$ (................, ...)   (1 mark)

2 Decide whether this statement is **true** or **false**:
'The line $2x - y = 6$ intersects with the circle $x^2 + y^2 = 17$ at the point (1, -4).'
Explain your reasoning.

_____

_____

(2 marks)

Score   / 7

Answer all parts of the questions. Show your workings (on a separate sheet of paper if necessary) and include the correct units in your answers.

1 a) Solve these simultaneous equations.

$x + 3y = -12$

$x^2 + y^2 = 34$

(5 marks)

b) Give a geometrical explanation of the result.

(2 marks)

2 The graph of $y = f(x)$ is sketched on the two grids below.

a) Sketch the graph of $y = f(-x)$ on this grid.

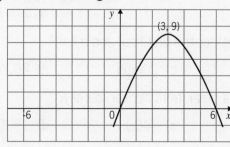

(2 marks)

b) Sketch the graph of $y = f(x + 2)$ on this grid.

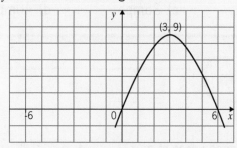

(2 marks)

3 The curve with equation $y = f(x)$ is translated so that the point at (0, 0) is mapped onto the point (-6, 0). Find the equation of the translated curve.

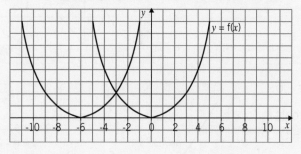

(2 marks)

Score   / 13

How well did you do?

0–5 **Try again**   6–10 **Getting there**   11–17 **Good work**   18–24 **Excellent!**

Algebra

For more information on this topic, see pages 50–51 of your Success Revision Guide.

Interpreting graphs

Multiple-choice questions

Choose just one answer, a, b, c or d. Circle your choice.

Use the graph opposite for these questions.
The graph represents Mrs Morgan's car journey.

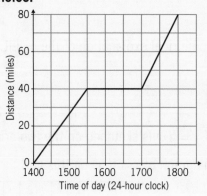

1 At what speed did Mrs Morgan travel for the first hour and a half?

    a) 25mph   **b)** 28mph   **c)** 30mph   **d)** 26.7mph   (1 mark)

2 At what time did Mrs Morgan take a break from her car journey?

    a) 1530   **b)** 1600   **c)** 1400   **d)** 1500   (1 mark)

3 At what speed did Mrs Morgan travel between 1700 and 1800 hours?

    a) 60mph   **b)** 80mph   **c)** 35mph   **d)** 40mph   (1 mark)

Score   / 3

Short-answer questions

Answer all parts of each question.

1 Water is poured into these odd-shaped vases at a constant rate. Match each vase to the correct graph.

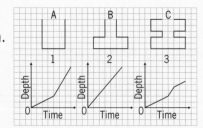

Vase A matches graph ....

Vase B matches graph ....

Vase C matches graph ....   (3 marks)

2 This is the graph of $y = x^2 - x - 6$.

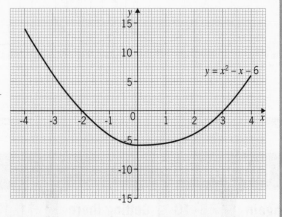

   a) Use the graph to find the roots of the equation $x^2 - x - 6 = 0$.

     .... and ....   (2 marks)

   b) By drawing suitable straight lines on the graph, solve these equations:

     i) $x^2 - x - 6 = 2$ ....   (2 marks)

     ii) $x^2 - 7 = 0$ ....   (3 marks)

Score   / 10

Answer all parts of the questions. Show your workings (on a separate sheet of paper if necessary) and include the correct units in your answers.

1 The graph shows how the value of a new car changed over a number of years.

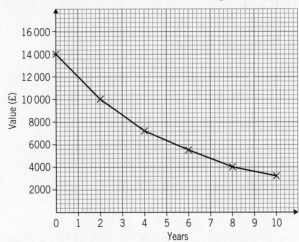

a) What was the price of the car when it was first bought? _____ **(1 mark)**

b) After how many years (to the nearest year) was the car worth 50% of its original value?

_____ **(1 mark)**

c) Robert said, 'The value of the car depreciated in value by approximately 71% after eight years.' Is Robert correct? Justify your answer. 🔲

_____ **(2 marks)**

d) Explain why the graph might be unsuitable for estimating the value of the car after 20 years.

_____

_____ **(2 marks)**

2 The sketch graph shows a curve $y = ab^x$ where $b > 0$.

The curve passes through the points (1, 6) and (3, 54).
Calculate the values of a and b.

$a = $ _____

$b = $ _____ **(3 marks)**

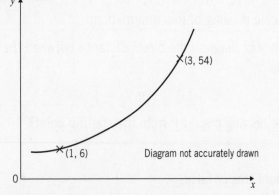

Diagram not accurately drawn

Algebra

Score   / 9

How well did you do?

| 0–5 | Try again | 6–10 | Getting there | 11–16 | Good work | 17–22 | Excellent! |

For more information on this topic, see pages 52–53 of your Success Revision Guide.

43

Bearings & scale drawings

Multiple-choice questions

Choose just one answer, a, b, c or d. Circle your choice.

1 The bearing of P from Q is 050°. What is the bearing of Q from P?

a) 130°   **b)** 50°   **c)** 230°   **d)** 310°   (1 mark)

2 The bearing of R from S is 130°. What is the bearing of S from R?

a) 310°   **b)** 230°   **c)** 050°   **d)** 200°   (1 mark)

3 The bearing of A from B is 240°. What is the bearing of B from A?

a) 120°   **b)** 60°   **c)** 320°   **d)** 060°   (1 mark)

4 The length of a car park is 25 metres. A scale diagram of the car park is being drawn to a scale of 1cm to 5 metres. What is the length of the car park on the scale diagram?

a) 500mm   **b)** 5cm   **c)** 50cm   **d)** 5m   (1 mark)

Score   / 4

Short-answer questions

Answer all parts of each question.

1 The scale on a road map is 1 : 50 000. Two towns are 20cm apart on the map. Work out the real distance, in km, between the two towns.

_____

(2 marks)

2 A ship sails on a bearing of 065° for 10km. It then continues on a bearing of 120° for a further 15km to a port (P).

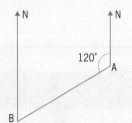

a) On a separate piece of paper, draw, using a scale of 1cm to 2km, an accurate scale drawing of this information.

(3 marks)

b) Measure on your diagram the direct distance between the starting point and port P.

_____ km

(1 mark)

c) What is the bearing of port P from the starting point?

_____ °

(1 mark)

3 Is this statement **true** or **false**?

'The bearing of B from A is 060°.'

_____

(1 mark)

Score   / 8

44

Answer all parts of the questions. Show your workings (on a separate sheet of paper if necessary) and include the correct units in your answers.

1 Here is a sketch of a triangle. Use a pair of compasses and a ruler to make an accurate scale drawing of the triangle on a separate sheet of paper. Use a scale of 1cm to 2m.

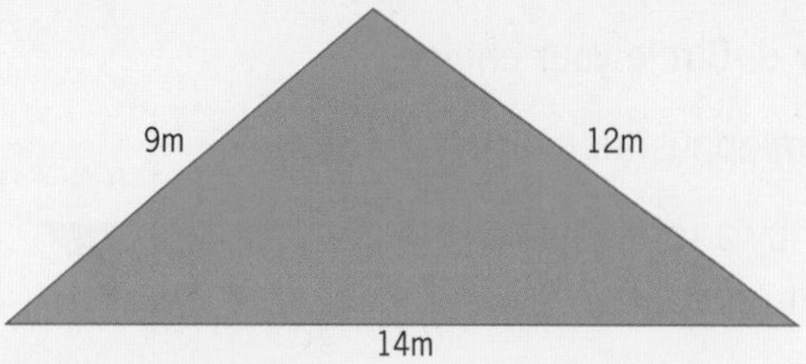

9m   12m

14m

(3 marks)

2 The scale drawing shows the positions of points A, B, C and D.
Point C is due east of point A.

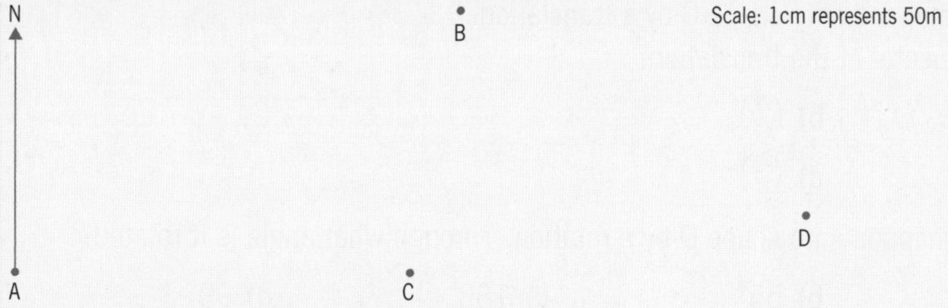

N

B

Scale: 1cm represents 50m

D

A   C

a) Use measurements from the drawing to find...

 i) the distance, in metres, of B from A _____ m   (1 mark)

 ii) the bearing of B from A _____ °   (2 marks)

 iii) the bearing of D from B. _____ °   (2 marks)

b) Point E is 250m from point C on a bearing of 055°. Mark the position of point E on the diagram above.   (2 marks)

3 The diagram shows the position of two buoys, A and B.

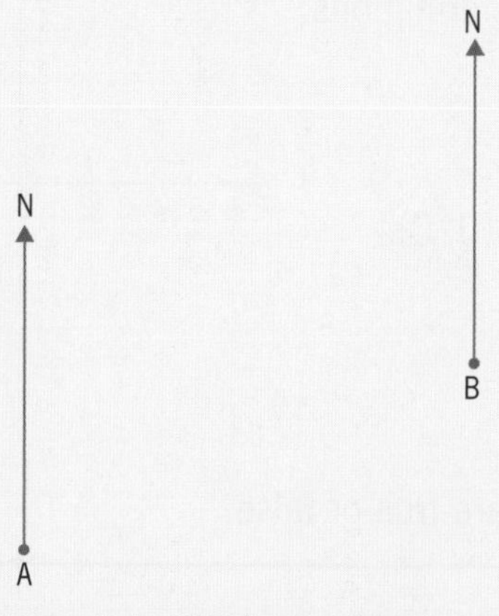

N

N

B

A

The bearing of buoy T from buoy A is 040°. The bearing of buoy T from buoy B is 260°. On the diagram above, show the position of buoy T.   (3 marks)

Score   / 13

How well did you do?

| 0–4 | Try again | 5–11 | Getting there | 12–18 | Good work | 19–25 | Excellent! |

For more information on this topic, see pages 60–61 of your Success Revision Guide.

Transformations 1

Multiple-choice questions

Choose just one answer, a, b, c or d. Circle your choice.

Questions 1–4 refer to the diagram opposite.

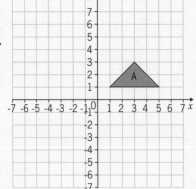

1 Shape A is mapped onto shape B by a reflection.
What is the equation of the line of reflection?

   a) $y = 1$ **b)** $x = 2$

   c) $y = x$ **d)** $y = -x$ **(1 mark)**

2 Shape A is mapped onto shape C by a translation.
What is the vector of the translation?

   a) $\binom{3}{7}$ **b)** $\binom{-7}{-3}$

   c) $\binom{7}{3}$ **d)** $\binom{-3}{-7}$ **(1 mark)**

3 Shape A is mapped onto shape D by a rotation. Through what angle is it rotated?

   a) 110°   **b)** 55°   **c)** 180°   **d)** 90°   **(1 mark)**

4 What special name is given to the relationship between triangles A, B, C and D?

   a) Enlargement   **b)** Congruent   **c)** Translation   **d)** Similar   **(1 mark)**

Score   / 4

Short-answer questions

Answer all parts of each question.

1 On the grid, carry out the following transformations.

   a) Reflect shape A in the y-axis.
       Call the new shape R.   **(1 mark)**

   b) Rotate shape A 90° clockwise, about (0, 0).
       Call the new shape S.   **(1 mark)**

   c) Translate shape A by the vector $\binom{-3}{4}$.
       Call the new shape T.   **(1 mark)**

2 State whether the following statements are **true** or **false**.

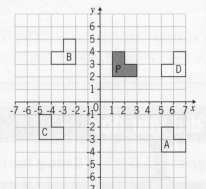

   a) Shape P can be transformed
       to shape A by a translation. _____   **(1 mark)**

   b) Shape P can be transformed
       to shape B by a rotation. _____   **(1 mark)**

   c) Shape P can be transformed
       to shape C by a reflection. _____   **(1 mark)**

   d) Shape P can be transformed
       to shape D by a reflection. _____   **(1 mark)**

Score   / 7

GCSE-style questions

Answer all parts of the questions. Show your workings (on a separate sheet of paper if necessary) and include the correct units in your answers.

1

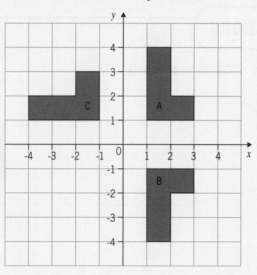

a) Describe fully the single transformation that takes shape A onto shape B.

....

....

(2 marks)

b) Describe fully the single transformation that takes shape A onto shape C.

....

....

(3 marks)

2

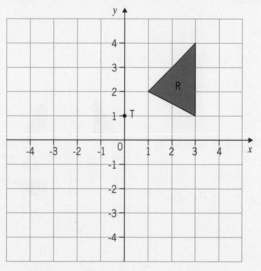

The triangle R has been drawn on the grid.

a) Rotate triangle R 90° clockwise about the point T (0, 1) and call the image P. (3 marks)

b) Translate triangle R by the vector $\begin{pmatrix} -4 \\ -3 \end{pmatrix}$ and call the image Q. (3 marks)

Score   / 11

How well did you do?

| 0–6 | Try again | 7–10 | Getting there | 11–16 | Good work | 17–22 | Excellent! |

For more information on this topic, see pages 62–65 of your Success Revision Guide.

Transformations 2

Multiple-choice questions

Choose just one answer, a, b, c or d. Circle your choice.

Questions 1–3 refer to the diagram opposite.

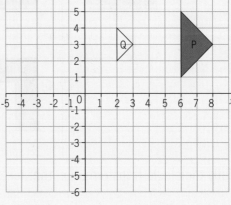

1 Shape P is enlarged to give shape Q.
What is the scale factor of the enlargement?

a) $\frac{1}{3}$　　　　　b) 2

c) 3　　　　　d) $\frac{1}{2}$

(1 mark)

2 Shape Q is enlarged to give shape P.
What is the scale factor of the enlargement?

a) $\frac{1}{3}$　　　　　b) 2

c) 3　　　　　d) $\frac{1}{2}$

(1 mark)

3 What are the coordinates of the centre of enlargement in both cases?

a) (3, -2)　　　b) (-2, 3)　　　c) (-3, 4)　　　d) (0, 0)

(1 mark)

Score　/ 3

Short-answer questions

Answer all parts of each question.

1 The diagram shows the position of three shapes, A, B and C.

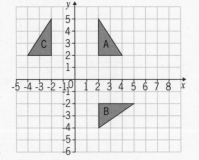

a) Describe the transformation that maps A onto C.

_____

(2 marks)

b) Describe the transformation that maps A onto B.

(2 marks)

c) Describe the transformation that maps B onto C.

(2 marks)

2 On the grid, enlarge
triangle PQR by a
scale factor of -2 with
centre of enlargement
(0, 0) and call the
image P'Q'R'.

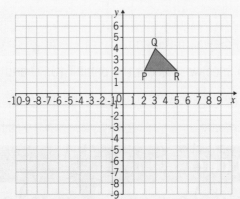

(3 marks)

Score　/ 9

48

GCSE Success

Maths
Higher Tier

Fiona Mapp

Answers

Number

Page 6 – Fractions

Multiple-choice questions
1. a
2. c
3. b
4. c
5. a

Short-answer questions
1. a) True
   b) False
2. 28 students
3. a) $\frac{5}{9}$
   b) $\frac{17}{44}$
   c) $\frac{3}{14}$
   d) 3
   e) $1\frac{2}{3}$
   f) $\frac{5}{9}$
   g) $\frac{7}{8}$
   h) $2\frac{34}{49}$
4. a) $\frac{1}{7}$ $\frac{3}{10}$ $\frac{1}{2}$ $\frac{2}{3}$ $\frac{3}{4}$ $\frac{4}{5}$
   b) $\frac{1}{9}$ $\frac{2}{7}$ $\frac{1}{3}$ $\frac{2}{5}$ $\frac{5}{8}$ $\frac{3}{4}$

GCSE-style questions
1. a) $\frac{8}{63}$
   b) $1\frac{16}{33}$
2. $\frac{7}{15}$
3. $\frac{1}{4} + \frac{1}{6} = \frac{6}{24} + \frac{4}{24} = \frac{10}{24}$
   $\frac{10}{24} \times \frac{1}{2} = \frac{5}{24}$ which is not $\frac{1}{5}$
4. $1 - \left(\frac{1}{3} + \frac{1}{8}\right) = 1 - \left(\frac{11}{24}\right)$
   Left $= \frac{13}{24} \div 4$
   Each child receives $\frac{13}{96}$
5. 13 sweets

Page 8 – Approximations & using a calculator

Multiple-choice questions
1. b
2. d
3. c
4. c
5. d

Short-answer questions
1. a) True
   b) False
   c) False
   d) True
2. a) 365
   b) 10.2
   c) 6320
   d) 0.0812
3. a) 100
   b) 90

GCSE-style questions
1. a) Vinson Massif
      Carstensz Pyramid
   b) 8850 – 4884 ≈
      8900 – 4900. Hence Gareth
      is correct because the
      difference in height is
      approximately 4000m.
2. a) 5.937 102 47...
   b) $\frac{30 \times 6}{40 - 10} = \frac{180}{30} = 6$
3. a) -856.859 649...
   b) -857
4. $\frac{125}{3}$

Page 10 – Percentages 1

Multiple-choice questions
1. c
2. c
3. a
4. d
5. b

Short-answer questions
1. a) £18
   b) £45
   c) £4
   d) 5g
2. £26 265
3. 40%
4. 77.3%
5. £20
6. £225
7. 39.3%

GCSE-style questions
1. Mileage per year = 7320. Fuel
   needed = 915 litres. Cost of
   fuel = £946.11. Percentage of
   annual salary = 5.1%
2. £8712
3. 20%
4. £70

Page 12 – Percentages 2

Multiple-choice questions
1. d
2. a
3. c
4. b

Short-answer questions
1. £75.60
2. £6969.60
3. £515.88
4. £135 475
5. 111.3p

GCSE-style questions
1. The sale price is 80% of the
   original price. 'Terrific Tuesday'
   is 80% of 80% = 64% not 60%.
2. £3.20 more with Nest Egg
3. £1337.11
4. $\frac{37\,246}{0.4} = £93\,115$
   $0.5 \times £93\,115 = £46\,557.50$
5. £11 340
6. £7874.05
7. a) 4.5%
   b) £59 728.23

Page 14 – Fractions, decimals & percentages

Multiple-choice questions
1. c
2. b
3. a
4. d
5. d

Short-answer questions
1.

Fraction	Decimal	Percentage
$\frac{2}{5}$	**0.4**	**40%**
$\frac{1}{20}$	**0.05**	5%
$\frac{1}{3}$	$0.\dot{3}$	**33.3%**
$\frac{1}{25}$	**0.04**	**4%**
$\frac{1}{4}$	**0.25**	25%
$\frac{1}{8}$	**0.125**	**12.5%**

2. Both will give the same answer
   because increasing by 20% is
   the same as multiplying by 1.2.
   Finding 10% then doubling it
   gives 20%, which when you
   add it to 40, is the same as
   increasing £40 by 20%.

GCSE-style questions
1. $\frac{1}{10}, \frac{3}{5}, \frac{5}{8}, \frac{2}{3}, \frac{9}{10}$
2. $\frac{1}{8}$, 25%, 0.27, $\frac{1}{3}$, $\frac{2}{5}$, 0.571,
   72%
3. Rosebushes is cheaper because
   $\frac{1}{4}$ = 25%, which is greater than
   the offer at Gardens Are Us.
4. a) Ed's Electricals: £225
      Sheila's Bargains: £217.38
      Gita's TV shop: £232
      She should buy from Sheila's
      Bargains and save £14.62
      over the most expensive shop.
   b) £200

Page 16 – Recurring decimals & surds

Multiple-choice questions
1. b
2. a
3. c
4. d
5. a

Short-answer questions
1. a) $2\sqrt{6}$
   b) $5\sqrt{3}$
   c) $6\sqrt{3}$
   d) $6\sqrt{5}$
2. $\frac{3\sqrt{2}}{2}$
3.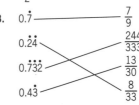

4. $\frac{124}{990} = \frac{62}{495}$

GCSE-style questions
1. a) 9
   b) $a = 4$
   c) $\frac{\sqrt{3} + \sqrt{12}}{\sqrt{75}}$
      $= \frac{\sqrt{3} + 2\sqrt{3}}{5\sqrt{3}}$
      $= \frac{3\sqrt{3}}{5\sqrt{3}} = \frac{3}{5}$
   d) $\frac{\sqrt{3}}{3}$
2. $\frac{(5 + \sqrt{5})(2 - 2\sqrt{5})}{\sqrt{45}}$
   $= \frac{10 - 10\sqrt{5} + 2\sqrt{5} - 2(\sqrt{5})^2}{3\sqrt{5}}$
   $= \frac{-8\sqrt{5}}{3\sqrt{5}} = \frac{-8}{3} = -2\frac{2}{3}$
3. $19 - 8\sqrt{3}$
4. $\frac{\sqrt{125} + \sqrt{50}}{\sqrt{5}}$
   $\frac{5\sqrt{5} + 5\sqrt{2}}{\sqrt{5}}$
   $\frac{5\sqrt{5} + 5\sqrt{2}}{\sqrt{5}} \times \frac{\sqrt{5}}{\sqrt{5}}$
   $\frac{5(\sqrt{5})^2 + 5\sqrt{10}}{5}$
   $= 5 + \sqrt{10}$
5. $1 + \sqrt{2}$
6. $\frac{2\sqrt{3} - 5}{\sqrt{3}} \times \frac{\sqrt{3}}{\sqrt{3}}$
   $= \frac{2 \times (\sqrt{3})^2 - 5\sqrt{3}}{(\sqrt{3})^2}$
   $= \frac{6 - 5\sqrt{3}}{3} = 2 - \frac{5\sqrt{3}}{3}$
7.

$\sqrt{\frac{1}{49}}$	$\frac{\sqrt{18}}{\sqrt{2}}$	$\sqrt{12}$	$\sqrt{16} - \sqrt{4}$	$\sqrt{3.6}$
✔	✔		✔	

8. a) $\frac{6}{11}$
   b) $\frac{26}{990} = \frac{13}{495}$
9. $\frac{61}{495}$
10. $\frac{7}{9}$
11. $0.\dot{4}\dot{5} = \frac{5}{11}$
    $x = 0.454\,545...$
    $100x = 45.454\,545...$
    $99x = 45$
    $x = \frac{45}{99}$
    $x = \frac{5}{11}$

Page 18 – Ratio

Multiple-choice questions
1. c
2. d
3. c
4. d
5. b

Short-answer questions
1. 1 : 1.5
2. 4.5 days

3. a) £10.25
 b) 48g
4. £25 000
5. 1200ml
6. £666.06

GCSE-style questions
1. Vicky: £6400; Tracy: £8000
2. 75g
3. 14 staff
4. a) $1237.50
 b) 164.43
5. £10.14
6. Small tin: cost per gram = $\frac{24}{142}$
 = 0.169p
 Large tin: cost per gram = $\frac{49}{300}$
 = 0.16\.{3}p
 Or: small tin = 5.916g per pence
 large tin = 6.122g per pence
 The large tin is better value.

Page 20 – Indices

Multiple-choice questions
1. a
2. b
3. c
4. d
5. a

Short-answer questions
1. a) $\frac{1}{5}$
 b) 343
 c) $\frac{25}{16}$
 d) $\frac{1}{27}$
2. a) False
 b) False
 c) True
 d) False
 e) False
 f) True
3. a) 1
 b) $16a^8$
 c) $\frac{3}{4}a^{-3}$ or $\frac{3}{4a^3}$
 d) $27a^6b^9$
4. a) $4x^{-2}$
 b) a^2b^{-3}
 c) $3y^{-5}$

GCSE-style questions
1. Hannah is wrong because
 $3m^4 \times 5m^6 = 3 \times 5 \times m^4 \times m^6$
 $= 15 \times m^{10} = 15m^{10}$
 Hannah has added the 5 and 3
 instead of multiplying them.
2. a) 1
 b) $\frac{1}{81}$
 c) 648
 d) 16
 e) $\frac{1}{5}$
3. a) i) 1
 ii) $\frac{1}{16}$
 iii) $\frac{3}{2} = 1\frac{1}{2}$
 b) 5^4
4. a) $\frac{1}{125}$
 b) $\frac{9}{4}$
 c) $\frac{1}{4}$

5. a) 2^{-1}
 b) 2^{20}
 c) $2^{\frac{5}{2}}$
6. a) p^7
 b) n^{-4} or $\frac{1}{n^4}$
 c) a^6
 d) $4ab$
7. a) $125x^3$
 b) y^{20}
 c) $\frac{1}{(3y)^3} = \frac{1}{27y^3}$ or $\frac{1}{27}y^{-3}$
 d) $32x^5y^{15}$

Page 22 – Standard index form

Multiple-choice questions
1. b
2. b
3. a
4. b
5. b

Short-answer questions
1. a) True
 b) False
 c) False
 d) False
2. a) 6×10^9
 b) 1.4×10^4
 c) 3×10^{16}
3. a) 8.19×10^3
 b) 7.56×10^2
 c) 6×10^{-7}
4. 1.8×10^{-7} grams

GCSE-style questions
1. a) i) 207 000
 ii) 4.6×10^{-5}
 b) 3.5×10^{12}
2. 9.54×10^5 seeds
3. 1.25×10^{-10}
4. 9.3×10^4
5. a) £8.6×10^5
 b) £6.2×10^5
6. 7200g

Page 24 – Upper & lower bounds of measurement

Multiple-choice questions
1. b
2. c
3. c
4. b
5. d

Short-answer questions
1. a) 111.5g
 b) 112.5g
2. Lower bound: E
 Upper bound: A
3. 11.25cm²

GCSE-style questions
1. a) 7.9cm
 b) 0.642cm
2. 0.886m
3. The upper bound for Jaydn's
 petrol consumption is
 $\frac{146.5}{15.55}$ = 9.42 miles per litre,
 so Jaydn's claim is almost
 certainly not correct.
4. Lower bound = 3.9717cm
 Upper bound = 3.9738cm
5. 10.5%

Algebra

Page 26 – Algebra & formulae

Multiple-choice questions
1. d
2. d
3. c
4. c
5. a

Short-answer questions
1. $T = 6b + 0.67p$ or $600b + 67p$
2. a) $5(2n + 3)$
 b) $12(2 - 3n)$
 c) $(n + 1)(n + 5)$
 d) $(n - 8)(n + 8)$
 e) $(n + 1)(n - 4)$
3. a) 4
 b) 5
 c) 8
4. a) $b = \frac{p + 4}{3}$
 b) $b = \pm\sqrt{4y + 6}$
 c) $b = \frac{2 - 5n}{3}$

GCSE-style questions
1. a) $4x + 7$
 b) i) $6(a + 2)$
 ii) $5a(2a - 3b)$
 c) i) $(n + 2)(n + 3)$
 ii) $\frac{2}{n + 2}$
 d) $(x + y)(x + y - 2)$
2. $(n - 1)^2 + n + (n - 1)$
 $= n^2 - 2n + 1 + n + n - 1$
 $= n^2 - 2n + 1 + 2n - 1$
 $= n^2$
3. $\frac{x^2 - 8x}{x^2 - 9x + 8} = \frac{x(x - 8)}{(x - 8)(x - 1)}$
 $= \frac{x}{(x - 1)}$
4. $(n) + (n + 1)$
 Let n be any whole number.
 $= 2n + 1$
 Sum of two consecutive
 numbers.
 Since $2n$ is always even, then
 $2n + 1$ will always be odd.
5. $b = \frac{89.5}{1.84^2}$
 $b = 26.435$, so yes, Peter is
 classed as overweight.

Page 28 – Equations

Multiple-choice questions
1. c
2. d
3. b
4. c
5. c

Short-answer questions
1. a) $n = 5$
 b) $n = 36$
 c) $n = 7$
 d) $n = -5.5$
 e) $n = 25$
 f) $n = 4$
2. a) $n = 3$
 b) $n = 5$
 c) $n = 4$
 d) $n = 14$
3. a) $n = 0, n = 4$
 b) $n = -5, n = -1$
 c) $n = 3, n = 2$
 d) $n = -4, n = 7$

4. $2n + (n + 30°) + (n - 10°) = 180°$
 $4n + 20° = 180°$
 $n = 40°$

GCSE-style questions
1. a) $m = 3$
 b) $p = \frac{6}{10}$ or $p = \frac{3}{5}$ or $p = 0.6$
 c) $x = 6$
 d) $\frac{3w + 2(3w + 2)}{6} = \frac{1}{3}$
 $3w + 6w + 4 = \frac{6}{3}$
 $3w + 6w + 4 = 2$
 $9w + 4 = 2$
 $w = -\frac{2}{9}$
2. a) $p = 2$
 b) $y = -\frac{10}{3}$ or $y = -3\frac{1}{3}$ or
 $y = -3.\dot{3}$
3. 17cm
4. $x = 1$ and $x = 3$
5. 110°

Page 30 – Equations & inequalities

Multiple-choice questions
1. a
2. d
3. c
4. d
5. c

Short-answer questions
1. a) $a = 2, b = 4$
 b) $a = 3, b = 9$
 c) $a = 3, b = -2$
2. 5.6
3. a) $x < 2$
 b) $x \geqslant 6$
 c) $1 \leqslant x \leqslant 4$
 d) $\frac{1}{3} < x \leqslant 2$

GCSE-style questions
1. a) -3, -2, -1, 0, 1, 2
 b) $p \leqslant 2$
2. $x = 2.7$ (You must show the full
 trial and improvement method
 in order to get full marks.)
3. $x = -3, y = 1.5$
4. Adult = £11.25 and
 child = £7.50
5.

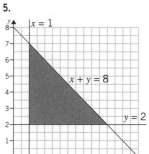

Page 32 – Advanced algebra & equations

Multiple-choice questions
1. c
2. c
3. d
4. b
5. a

Short-answer questions

1. **a)** $(x + 6)(x + 5)$

   b) $\dfrac{4}{(x + 6)} + \dfrac{4}{(x^2 + 11x + 30)}$

   $= \dfrac{4}{(x + 6)} + \dfrac{4}{(x + 6)(x + 5)}$

   $= \dfrac{4(x + 5) + 4}{(x + 6)(x + 5)}$

   $= \dfrac{4x + 24}{(x + 6)(x + 5)}$

   $= \dfrac{4(x + 6)}{(x + 6)(x + 5)}$

   $= \dfrac{4}{(x + 5)}$

2. **a)** $(x + 4)(x - 3) = 2$

   $x^2 + x - 12 = 2$

   $x^2 + x - 14 = 0$

   b) $x = 3.27$ or $x = -4.27$

3. $a = \dfrac{3(b + c)}{bc}$

   $abc = 3b + 3c$

   $abc - 3c = 3b$

   $c(ab - 3) = 3b$

   Therefore $c = \dfrac{3b}{ab - 3}$

   Greg is right.

GCSE-style questions

1. **a)** $a = 3$, $b = -6$

   b) Minimum value is -6.

2. $a = \dfrac{8b + 5}{4 - 3b}$

   $a(4 - 3b) = 8b + 5$

   $4a - 3ab = 8b + 5$

   $4a - 5 = 8b + 3ab$

   $4a - 5 = b(8 + 3a)$

   $b = \dfrac{4a - 5}{8 + 3a}$

3. **a)** $\dfrac{1}{2} \times (x - 3) \times (x + 4) = 12$

   $(x - 3)(x + 4) = 24$

   $x^2 + x - 12 = 24$

   $x^2 + x - 36 = 0$

   b) $x = 5.52$cm

   Therefore the base of the triangle is 2.52cm.

4. $P = 4a + \pi a + 3b$

   $P - 3b = 4a + \pi a$

   $P - 3b = a(4 + \pi)$

   $a = \dfrac{P - 3b}{4 + \pi}$

5. $x = 4.21$ or $x = -0.712$

Page 34 – Direct & inverse proportion

Multiple-choice questions

1. d
2. a
3. b
4. c

Short-answer questions

1.

x	2	4	3	5
y	12	48	27	75

2. **a)** $z = \dfrac{k}{v^2}$

   b) i) 62.5

   ii) $\pm\dfrac{1}{2}$

3. 5

GCSE-style questions

1. 324
2. $E = kF$

   $6 = k \times 15$

   $\therefore k = \dfrac{2}{5}$

   $E = \dfrac{2}{5}F$

   When $F = 80$N, $E = 32$cm

3. $V = kh^3$

   $60 = k \times 8$

   $k = 7.5$

   $V = 7.5h^3$

   $V = 937.5$cm³

4. **a)** $I = \dfrac{k}{d^2}$

   $50 = \dfrac{k}{4}$

   $\therefore k = 200$

   $I = \dfrac{200}{d^2}$

   $I = 16.3$

   b) $d = 4$

5. $f \propto \dfrac{1}{w}$

   $f = \dfrac{k}{w}$

   $45 = \dfrac{k}{16.2}$

   $k = 729$

   $f = \dfrac{729}{w}$

   $w = \dfrac{729}{24}$

   $w = 30.375$m

6. $c = \dfrac{k}{b}$

   $\therefore 4 = \dfrac{k}{10}$ so $k = 40$

   Daisy is correct.

Page 36 – Straight-line graphs

Multiple-choice questions

1. b
2. d
3. b
4. c
5. a

Short-answer questions

1. **a)–b) i)**

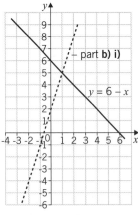

   ii) $y = 3x + 2$

   c) (1, 5)

2. $y = 3 - 2x$ and $y = 4 - 2x$

GCSE-style questions

1. (-2, -10), (1, -1) and (0, -4) should be ticked.

---

2. **a)**

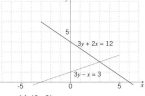

   b) (3, 2)

   c) $-\dfrac{2}{3}$

   d) $3y + 2x = 6$ or $y = -\dfrac{2}{3}x + 2$

   e) $\dfrac{3}{2}$

Page 38 – Curved graphs

Multiple-choice questions

1. b
2. d
3. c
4. d
5. b

Short-answer questions

1. **a)**

x	-2	-1	0	1	2	3
$y = x^2 - 2x - 2$	6	1	-2	-3	-2	1

   b)

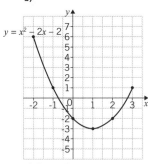

   c) i) $y = -3$

   ii) $x = 2.75$ and $x = -0.75$

GCSE-style questions

1. **a)**

x	-2	-1	0	1	2	3
$y = x^3 - 4$	-12	-5	-4	-3	4	23

   b)

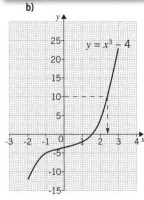

   c) i) $x = 1.6$

   ii) $x = 2.4$

   iii) $x = 1.8$

   iv) $x = -1.4$

Page 40 – Advanced graphs

Multiple-choice questions

1. c
2. a
3. d
4. c

Short-answer questions

1. **a)** (2, 4)

   b) (1, 7)

   c) (6, 7)

   d) (-2, 7)

   e) (1, 7)

2. The statement is true since $x = 1$, $y = -4$ is a simultaneous solution of the two equations:

   i.e. $2 \times 1 - (-4) = 6$

   $1^2 + (-4)^2 = 17$

GCSE-style questions

1. **a)** $x = 3$ or $x = -5\dfrac{2}{5}$

   $y = -5$ or $y = -2\dfrac{1}{5}$

   b) They are the coordinates of the points where the line $3y = -12 - x$ intersects with the circle $x^2 + y^2 = 34$.

2. **a)**

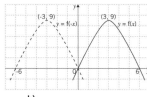

   b)

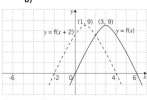

3. $y = f(x + 6)$

Page 42 – Interpreting graphs

Multiple-choice questions

1. d
2. a
3. d

Short-answer questions

1. Vase A – graph 2

   Vase B – graph 1

   Vase C – graph 3

2. **a)** $x = 3$ and $x = -2$ (read where the curve crosses the x-axis).

   b) i) Approximately, $x = 3.3$ and $x = -2.3$ (read across where $y = 2$).

   ii) Approximately, $x = -2.7$ and $x = 2.6$ (draw the line $y = 1 - x$ and find the point of intersection with the curve).

GCSE-style questions

1. **a)** £14 000

   b) 4 years

   c) % depreciation = $\dfrac{10\,000}{14\,000} \times 100\% = 71\%$

   Robert is correct.

d) The graph is presuming that the car will continue to decrease in value at the same rate and after 20 years it would be worth negative amounts of money, which is not the case. After 20 years, the car could still have a scrap value.

2. $a = 2$, $b = 3$

Geometry and measures

Page 44 – Bearings & scale drawings

Multiple-choice questions
1. c
2. a
3. d
4. b

Short-answer questions
1. 10km
2. **a)** Your diagram should have a scale of 1cm to 2km.

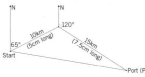

   b) 11.1cm = 22.2km (±0.2km)
   c) 098° (±1°)
3. False

GCSE-style questions
1. Your diagram should have a scale of 1cm to 2m. Lengths must be ± 2mm.

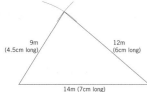

2. **a) i)** 325m
      ii) 060°
      iii) 120°
   b)

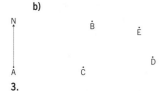

3.

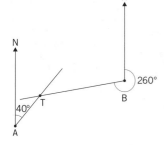

Page 46 – Transformations 1

Multiple-choice questions
1. c
2. d
3. d
4. b

Short-answer questions
1. **a)–c)**

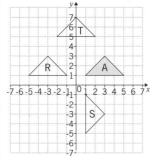

2. **a)** True
   b) True
   c) False
   d) True

GCSE-style questions
1. **a)** Reflection in the x-axis
   b) Rotation 90° anticlockwise about (0, 0)
2. **a)–b)**

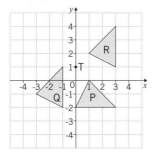

Page 48 – Transformations 2

Multiple-choice questions
1. d
2. b
3. b

Short-answer questions
1. **a)** Reflection in the y-axis
   b) Rotation 90° clockwise about (0, 0)
   c) Reflection in the line $y = x$
2.

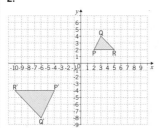

GCSE-style questions
1.

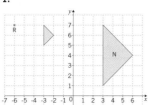

2. **a)** Translation by the vector $\begin{pmatrix} -12 \\ -7 \end{pmatrix}$
   b) Enlargement by a scale factor of $-\frac{1}{2}$, centre of enlargement at (0, 5)
   c) Reflection in the line $y = 0$ or x-axis

Page 50 – Similarity & congruency

Multiple-choice questions
1. c
2. b
3. a
4. b

Short-answer questions
1. **a)** $n = 8$cm
   b) $n = 6.\dot{6}$cm
   c) $n = 9.8$cm
2. **a)** Congruent (RHS)
   b) Not congruent
   c) Congruent (SSS)

GCSE-style questions
1. **a)** 5cm
   b) 15cm
2. RST and RUT are both isosceles triangles.
   Angle RST = Angle RUT
   Angle SRT = Angle URT
   Angle UTR = Angle STR
   Common length is RT.
   Since three angles and one side are the same, triangles RST and RUT are congruent, i.e. AAS.
   Or, all three lengths of both triangles are the same, hence SSS.
3. **a)** 450cm^2
   b) 1.08 litres

Page 52 – Loci & coordinates in 3D

Multiple-choice questions
1. c
2. d
3. a
4. d
5. b

Short-answer questions
1.

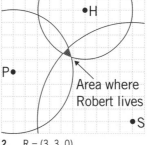

2. R = (3, 3, 0)
   S = (3, 1, 3)
   T = (0, 1, 3)
   U = (0, 1, 1)

GCSE-style questions
1.

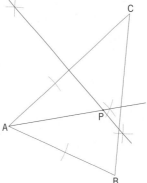

2. (5, 0, 3)

Page 54 – Angle properties of circles

Multiple-choice questions
1. c
2. a
3. d
4. a
5. c

Short-answer questions
1. **a)** $a = 65°$
   b) $a = 18°$
   c) $a = 60°$
   d) $a = 50°$
   e) $a = 82°$
2. John is correct. Angle a is 42° because angles in the same segment are equal.

GCSE-style questions
1. **a)** 140°
   b) 70°
2. 71°. Either alternate segment theorem or angle ABC is 90° because of angles in a semicircle. Angle ACB is 19° hence angles in a triangle add up to 180°, so BAC is 71°.
3. Billy is correct since angle OBC = 90° (tangent and radius meet at 90°) hence angle OBA = 90° − y. Since angle OBA = angle OAB, triangle AOB is isosceles. ∴ angle AOB = 180° − 2(90° − y) because angles in a triangle add up to 180°.
   = 180° − 180° + 2y
   = 2y

Page 56 – Pythagoras' theorem

Multiple-choice questions
1. c
2. d
3. b
4. a

Short-answer questions
1. Both statements are true. Length of line = $\sqrt{6^2 + 3^2}$ = $\sqrt{45}$ in surd form.
   Midpoint = $\frac{(2 + 5)}{2}$, $\frac{(5 + 11)}{2}$
   = (3.5, 8)
2. **a)** $n = 15$cm
   b) $n = 12.6$cm
   c) $n = 29.1$cm
   d) $n = 24.6$cm
3. Since $12^2 + 5^2 = 144 + 25 = 169 = 13^2$, the triangle must be right-angled for Pythagoras' theorem to be applied.

GCSE-style questions
1. 13.7m
2. $\sqrt{41}$ units
3. 48.6m
4. £13.52

Page 58 – Trigonometry in right-angled triangles

Multiple-choice questions
1. a
2. b
3. d
4. a
5. c

Short-answer questions
1. a) $n = 5$cm
   b) $n = 6.3$cm
   c) $n = 13.8$cm
   d) $n = 14.9$cm
   e) $n = 6.7$cm
2. a) 38.7°
   b) 52.5°
   c) 23.6°

GCSE-style questions
1. 15cm
2. 65°
3. 62.6cm²
4. 2.7m

Page 60 – Application of trigonometry

Multiple-choice questions
1. c
2. c
3. b

Short-answer questions
1. 068°
2. 13.8cm
3. a) i) True
      ii) True
   b) 40.9°

GCSE-style questions
1. 30.1°
2. 206°
3. a) 389.9m
   b) 14.6°
   c) Find angle SRT:

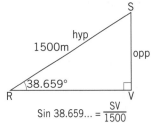

   $\text{Tan } x = \dfrac{\text{opp}}{\text{adj}} = \dfrac{1200}{1500}$

   $x = \tan^{-1} 0.8$
     $= 38.659...°$
   Find SV from triangle RSV:

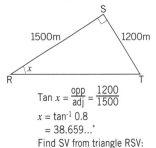

   $\text{Sin } 38.659... = \dfrac{SV}{1500}$

   $SV = 1500 \times \sin 38.659...$
     $= 937.042...$
   Find angle PVS from triangle PVS:

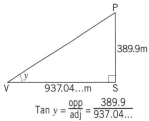

   $\text{Tan } y = \dfrac{\text{opp}}{\text{adj}} = \dfrac{389.9}{937.04...}$

   $y = \tan^{-1} 0.416...$
   Angle of elevation = 22.6°
4. 26.2cm

Page 62 – Further trigonometry

Multiple-choice questions
1. c
2. a
3. d
4. c

Short-answer questions
1. a) 13.2cm (3 s.f.)
   b) 17.3cm (3 s.f.)
   c) 32.5° (1 d.p.)
   d) 70.9° (1 d.p.)
2. Area $= \dfrac{1}{2} \times 18 \times 13 \times \sin 37°$

   $= 70.4$cm²
   Area is approximately 70cm².
   Isobel is correct.
3. a) A (0°, 1), B (90°, 0),
      C (270°, 0), D (360°, 1)
   b)

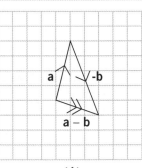

GCSE-style questions
1. a) 10.5cm
   b) 42.5cm²
2. 4.13cm
3. 44cm²

Page 64 – Measures & measurement

Multiple-choice questions
1. b
2. d
3. a
4. d
5. c

Short-answer questions
1. a) 8000m
   b) 3.25kg
   c) 7000kg
   d) 0.52m
   e) 2700ml
   f) 0.002 62km
2. 15 miles
3. 1.1 pounds
4. 50mph
5. 0.1g/cm⁻³
6. Upper limit = 47.5m
   Lower limit = 46.5m

GCSE-style questions
1. a) 17.6 pounds
   b) 48km
2. Length = 12.05cm
   Width = 5.5cm
3. a) 1 hour 36 minutes
   b) 4.4km/h
4. 80kg
5. Speed $= \dfrac{2400}{108} = 22.\dot{2}$m/s

   $\dfrac{22.\dot{2}}{4.47} = 4.97$

   4.97×10mph $= 49.7$mph
   The car was not speeding
   through the roadworks.

Page 66 – Area of 2D shapes

Multiple-choice questions
1. c
2. b
3. d
4. d

Short-answer questions
1. a) False
   b) False
   c) False
2. 85cm²
3. 38.6cm
4. 70 000cm²

GCSE-style questions
1. £33
2. £2170
3. 388m
4. 16cm

Page 68 – Volume of 3D shapes

Multiple-choice questions
1. a
2. c
3. c
4. d

Short-answer questions
1. 156cm²
2. Emily is not correct. The
   correct volume is 345.6 ÷ 2,
   i.e. 172.8m³.
3. 170.2m³
4. 9.9cm
5. 3807cm³

GCSE-style questions
1. 64cm³
2. a) 672cm³
   b) 3696g
3. £25.35
4. 3.2cm

Page 70 – Further length, area & volume

Multiple-choice questions
1. b
2. a
3. d
4. a
5. c

Short-answer questions
1. Solid A is 314cm³.
   Solid B is 600cm³.
   Solid C is 2145cm³.
   Solid D is 68cm³.
2. The statement is false because:
   Area of segment = area of
   sector – area of triangle
   = 13.09 – 10.83
   = 2.26cm²

GCSE-style questions
1. 26.5cm
2. 73°
3. 0.0248m³
4. 9 spheres

Page 72 – Vectors

Multiple-choice questions
1. b
2. c
3. a
4. b
5. b

Short-answer questions
1. a) True
   b) False
   c) True
   d) False

2. $\overrightarrow{OC} = 2\mathbf{a} - 3\mathbf{b}$,
   $\overrightarrow{OD} = 6(2\mathbf{a} - 3\mathbf{b})$
   Hence the vectors are parallel
   as one vector is a multiple of
   the other. The vectors lie on
   a straight line through O.

3.

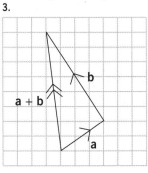

   a) $\mathbf{a} + \mathbf{b} = \begin{pmatrix} -1 \\ 8 \end{pmatrix}$

   b) $\mathbf{a} - \mathbf{b} = \begin{pmatrix} 3 \\ -1 \end{pmatrix}$

GCSE-style questions
1. $\begin{pmatrix} 2 \\ 4 \end{pmatrix}$

2. $\overrightarrow{AB} = -3\mathbf{a} + 3\mathbf{b}$,
   $\overrightarrow{CD} = -5\mathbf{a} + 5\mathbf{b}$
   Since $\overrightarrow{AB} = \dfrac{3}{5}\overrightarrow{CD}$, AB and CD
   are parallel.

3. a) $\overrightarrow{AC} = \mathbf{a} + \mathbf{b}$
   b) $\overrightarrow{BD} = \mathbf{b} + 2\mathbf{b} - \mathbf{a}$
      $= 3\mathbf{b} - \mathbf{a}$
      hence $\overrightarrow{AD} = \overrightarrow{AB} + \overrightarrow{BD}$
      $= \mathbf{a} + 3\mathbf{b} - \mathbf{a}$
      $\overrightarrow{AD} = 3\mathbf{b}$
      $\overrightarrow{AD} = 3\overrightarrow{BC}$, so BC is parallel
      to AD.
   c) $\overrightarrow{AN} = \overrightarrow{AD} + \overrightarrow{DN}$
      $= 3\mathbf{b} - \dfrac{1}{2}(2\mathbf{b} - \mathbf{a})$
      $= 3\mathbf{b} - \mathbf{b} + \dfrac{1}{2}\mathbf{a}$
      $= \dfrac{1}{2}\mathbf{a} + 2\mathbf{b}$
   d) $\overrightarrow{YD} = \overrightarrow{YA} + \overrightarrow{AD}$
      $= -\dfrac{3}{4}(\dfrac{1}{2}\mathbf{a} + 2\mathbf{b}) + 3\mathbf{b}$
      $= -\dfrac{3}{8}\mathbf{a} - \dfrac{3}{2}\mathbf{b} + 3\mathbf{b}$
      $= -\dfrac{3}{8}\mathbf{a} + \dfrac{3}{2}\mathbf{b}$
      $= \dfrac{3}{8}(4\mathbf{b} - \mathbf{a})$

Statistics and probability

Page 74 – Collecting data

Multiple-choice questions
1. b
2. a
3. d

Short-answer questions
1. The tick boxes overlap. Which box would somebody who did 2 hours of homework tick? It also needs extra boxes for more than 4 hours.
'How much time do you spend doing homework each night?'

0 up to 1 hour	1 up to 2 hours	2 up to 3 hours	3 up to 4 hours	4 up to 5 hours	5 hours or more

2.

Year group	Number of students	Number of students in sample
7	120	**15**
8	176	**22**
9	160	**20**
10	190	**24**
11	154	**19**

GCSE-style questions
1. a) The question is too vague – what is meant by 'a healthy diet'? The tick options are too vague – how often is 'sometimes'? 'Every day' and 'yes' could mean the same thing.
   b) Method 1, since all the patients have an equally likely chance of being chosen and this will avoid bias.
2. The key to this question is to break it into subgroups and a time frame, e.g. per day, per week, etc.
   On average, how many hours per school day do you spend watching television?
   0 up to 1 hour ☐
   1 up to 2 hours ☐
   2 up to 3 hours ☐
   3 up to 4 hours ☐
   More than 4 hours ☐
3. a) 30 students
   b) 14 girls

Page 76 – Scatter graphs & correlation

Multiple-choice questions
1. c
2. a
3. b

Short-answer questions
1. a) Positive correlation
   b) Negative correlation
   c) Positive correlation
   d) No correlation
2. a) Positive correlation
   b)

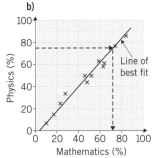

   c) Approximately 72%

GCSE-style questions
1. a)

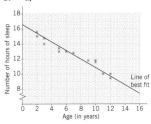

   b) Negative correlation – the younger the child, the more hours of sleep they had.
   c) See line of best fit on the graph above.
   d) A 4-year-old child has approximately 14 hours of sleep.
   e) This only gives an estimate as it follows the trend of the data. Similarly, if you continued the line it would assume that you may eventually need no hours of sleep at a certain age, which is not the case.
   f) The child psychologist is not correct. From the data, 5-year-old children have approximately 13 hours of sleep.

Page 78 – Averages 1

Multiple-choice questions
1. c
2. b
3. d

Short-answer questions
1. a) False
   b) True
   c) False
   d) True
2. a) 141.35 beans
   b) The manufacturer is justified in making this claim because the mean is just over 141, and the mode and median are also approximately 141.
3. $x = 17$

GCSE-style questions
1. a) 5
   b) 3
   c) 4.65
2. 81

3. £440
4. 9.4 adverts

Page 80 – Averages 2

Multiple-choice questions
1. c
2. b
3. a
4. a

Short-answer questions
1. 21.5mm
2. a) 47
   b) 35
   c) 40

GCSE-style questions
1. Median time for boys = 23 minutes
   Median time for girls = 29 minutes
   The median time for girls to solve the problem is greater than the median time for boys.
   Range for boys = 49 – 10 = 39 minutes
   Range for girls = 43 – 12 = 31 minutes
   The range for boys is greater than the range for girls.
   Interquartile range for boys = 38 – 17 = 21 minutes
   Interquartile range for girls = 33 – 17 = 16 minutes
   The interquartile range for girls is smaller than for boys.
2. a) £31.80
   b) This is only an estimate because the midpoints of the data have been used.
   c) $30 \leqslant x < 40$
   d) Although the modal class interval is $10 \leqslant x < 20$, since the mean is £31.80 and the median class interval is $30 \leqslant x < 40$, Edward's claim is not correct because the other averages indicate that the average amount spent is between £30 and £40.

Page 82 – Cumulative frequency graphs

Multiple-choice questions
1. c
2. d
3. a

Short-answer questions
1. a)

Examination mark	Frequency	Cumulative frequency
0–10	4	**4**
11–20	6	**10**
21–30	11	**21**
31–40	24	**45**
41–50	18	**63**
51–60	7	**70**
61–70	3	**73**

b)

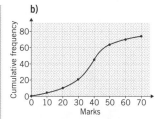

c) 43 – 27 = 16 marks
d) 45.5 marks

GCSE-style questions
1. a)

Time t (minutes)	Frequency	Cumulative frequency
$120 < t \leqslant 140$	1	**1**
$140 < t \leqslant 160$	8	**9**
$160 < t \leqslant 180$	24	**33**
$180 < t \leqslant 200$	29	**62**
$200 < t \leqslant 220$	10	**72**
$220 < t \leqslant 240$	5	**77**
$240 < t \leqslant 260$	3	**80**

b)

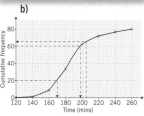

c) i) 198 – 170 = 28 minutes
   ii) 80 – 65 = 15 runners
d)

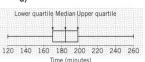

e) In the second marathon, the median time was lower and the interquartile range was greater (36 minutes as opposed to 28 minutes). All the runners had completed the marathon in 220 minutes or less as opposed to 260 minutes or less in the first marathon.

Page 84 – Histograms

Multiple-choice questions
1. d
2. b
3. b
4. a

Short-answer questions
1. a)

Time t (minutes)	Frequency
$0 < t \leqslant 5$	19
$5 < t \leqslant 15$	**26**
$15 < t \leqslant 20$	16
$20 < t \leqslant 30$	**14**
$30 < t \leqslant 45$	12

b)

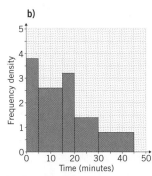

GCSE-style questions

1.

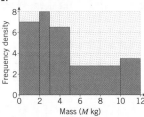

2.

Time S (seconds)	Frequency
$0 \leqslant S < 10$	**2**
$10 \leqslant S < 15$	**5**
$15 \leqslant S < 20$	21
$20 \leqslant S < 40$	**28**
$S \geqslant 40$	0

Page 86 – Probability

Multiple-choice questions
1. d
2. c
3. b
4. a
5. d

Short-answer questions
1. a) $\frac{4}{16} = \frac{1}{4}$
   b) $\frac{2}{16} = \frac{1}{8}$
   c) 0
2. 0.09

3. a) $\frac{7}{26}$
   b) $\frac{7}{13}$

GCSE-style questions
1. a) i) 0.35
      ii) 0
   b) 50 red beads
2. a) $\frac{6}{36} = \frac{1}{6}$
   b) $\frac{4}{36} = \frac{1}{9}$
3. a)

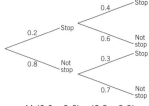

   b) $(0.2 \times 0.6) + (0.8 \times 0.3)$
   $= 0.12 + 0.24$
   $= 0.36$

GCSE-style questions

Answer all parts of the questions. Show your workings (on a separate sheet of paper if necessary) and include the correct units in your answers.

1 Enlarge triangle N by a scale factor of $\frac{1}{3}$ with centre R (-6, 7).

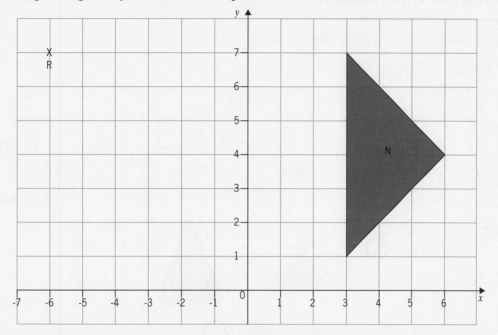

(3 marks)

2 The diagram shows four triangles, T_1, T_2, T_3 and T_4.

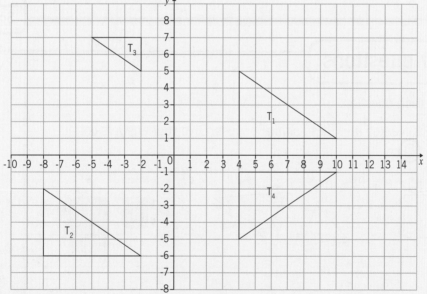

Describe fully the single transformation that maps...

a) T_1 onto T_2 _____ (2 marks)

b) T_1 onto T_3 _____ (2 marks)

c) T_1 onto T_4. _____ (2 marks)

Score / 9

How well did you do?

| 0–4 | Try again | 5–9 | Getting there | 10–16 | Good work | 17–21 | Excellent! |

For more information on this topic, see pages 62–65 of your Success Revision Guide.

Similarity & congruency

Multiple-choice questions

Choose just one answer, a, b, c or d. Circle your choice.

1 These two shapes are similar.
What is the size of angle x?

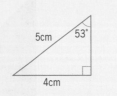

Diagrams not
accurately drawn

5cm 53°

4cm

15cm

x

y

a) 90°   b) 47°

c) 53°   d) 50°   (1 mark)

2 What is the length of y in the larger triangle above?

a) 14cm   b) 12cm   c) 8cm   d) 16cm   (1 mark)

3 These two shapes are similar. What is
the radius of the smaller cone?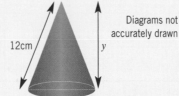

Diagrams not
accurately drawn

5cm 4cm 12cm y

$= x$

$= 7.2$cm

a) 3cm   b) 9.6cm

c) 5cm   d) 10cm   (1 mark)

4 What is the perpendicular height of the larger cone above?

a) 3cm   b) 9.6cm   c) 9cm   d) 12cm   (1 mark)

Score   / 4

Short-answer questions

Answer all parts of each question.

1 Calculate the lengths marked n in these similar shapes. Give your answers correct
to 1 decimal place.

a)   b)   c)

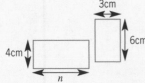

3cm

6cm

4cm

n

10cm

4cm

6cm

n

3.5cm n

5cm

14cm

$n =$ _____ cm $n =$ _____ cm $n =$ _____ cm   (6 marks)

2 Which of the following pairs of triangles, C and D, are congruent? For those that are,
state whether the reason is SSS, RHS, SAS or AAS.

a)   b)   c)

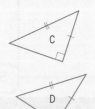

C

D

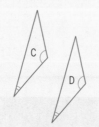

C

D

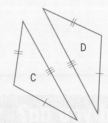

D

C

_____   _____   _____   (3 marks)

Score   / 9

GCSE-style questions

Answer all parts of the questions. Show your workings (on a separate sheet of paper if necessary) and include the correct units in your answers.

1 In the diagram, MN is parallel to YZ.
YMX and ZNX are straight lines.
XM = 4cm, XY = 14cm, XN = 6cm,
YZ = 17.5cm.

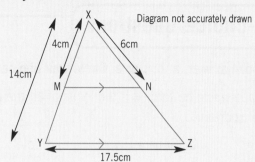

Diagram not accurately drawn

a) Calculate the length of MN. 🖩 ....

.... cm   (2 marks)

b) Calculate the length of NZ. 🖩 ....

.... cm   (2 marks)

2 In the diagram, RS = ST = RU = TU.
Prove that the triangle RST is
congruent to triangle RUT.

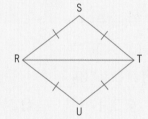

....

....

(3 marks)

3 Soup is sold in two similar cylindrical cans.

a) The area of the label on the smaller can is 162cm². Calculate the area of the label on the larger can. (The labels are also similar and in the same proportion as the height of the cans.) 🖩

.... cm²   (2 marks)

b) The capacity of the larger can of soup is 5 litres. Calculate the capacity of the smaller can of soup. 🖩

.... litres   (2 marks)

Score   / 11

How well did you do?

| 0–6 | Try again | 7–12 | Getting there | 13–18 | Good work | 19–24 | Excellent! |

For more information on this topic, see pages 66–67 of your Success Revision Guide.

51

Geometry and measures

Loci & coordinates in 3D

Multiple-choice questions

Choose just one answer, a, b, c or d. Circle your choice.

1 What 2D shape would be formed if the locus of all the points equidistant from a fixed point P is drawn?

   a) Rectangle   **b)** Square   **c)** Circle   **d)** Kite   **(1 mark)**

Questions 2–5 refer to the diagram below.

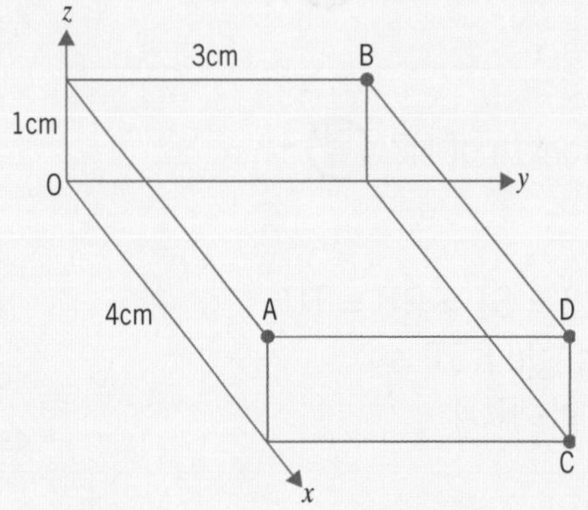

2 What are the coordinates of point A?

   a) (4, 3, 1)   **b)** (4, 3, 0)

   c) (0, 3, 1)   **d)** (4, 0, 1)   **(1 mark)**

3 What are the coordinates of point B?

   a) (0, 3, 1)   **b)** (0, 0, 0)

   c) (4, 3, 0)   **d)** (0, 3, 0)   **(1 mark)**

4 What are the coordinates of point C?

   a) (0, 3, 1)   **b)** (4, 3, 1)   **c)** (4, 0, 0)   **d)** (4, 3, 0)   **(1 mark)**

5 What are the coordinates of the midpoint of OC?

   a) (4, 3, 0)   **b)** (2, 1.5, 0)   **c)** (2, 1.5, 0.5)   **d)** (2, 0, 1.5)   **(1 mark)**

Score   / 5

Short-answer questions

Answer all parts of each question.

1 The diagram shows the position of the post office (P), the hospital (H) and the school (S). Robert lives less than 4 miles away from the hospital, less than 5 miles away from the post office and less than 8 miles away from the school. Use shading to show the area where Robert lives. Use a scale of 1 grid square = 1 mile.

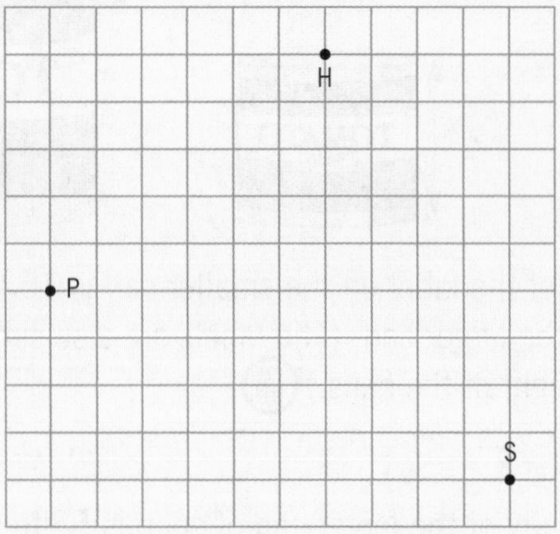

(4 marks)

2 The diagram shows a solid. Complete the coordinates for each of the vertices listed below.

   R = (_____, _____, _____)

   S = (_____, _____, _____)

   T = (_____, _____, _____)

   U = (_____, _____, _____)

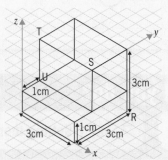

(4 marks)

Score   / 8

GCSE-style questions

Answer all parts of the questions. Show your workings (on a separate sheet of paper if necessary) and include the correct units in your answers.

1 In this question you should use a ruler and a pair of compasses only for the constructions.

Triangle ABC is the plan of an adventure playground.

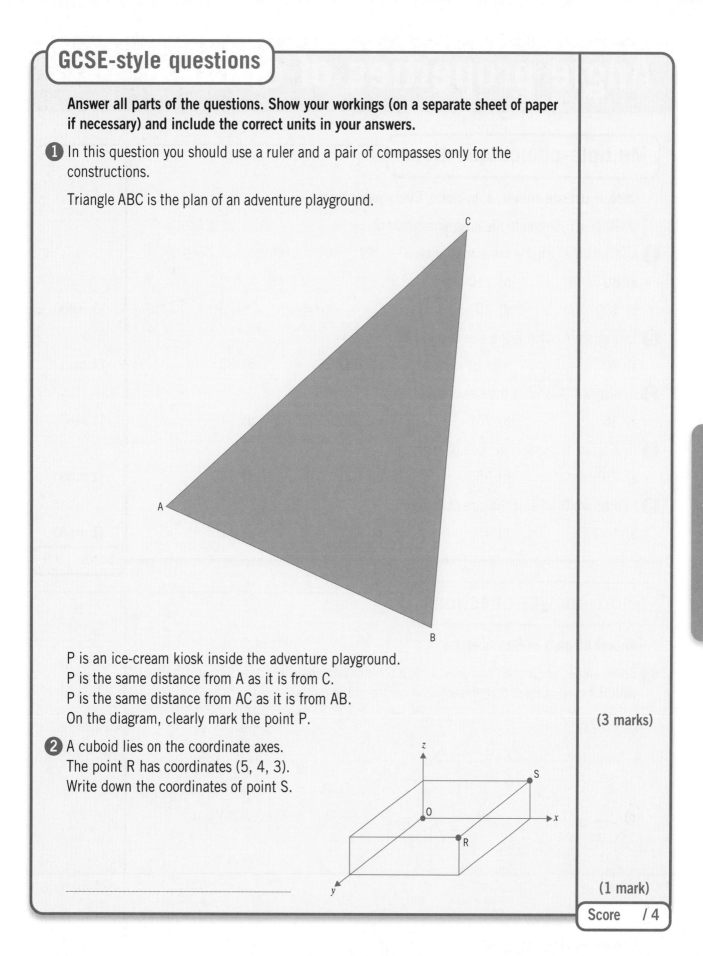

P is an ice-cream kiosk inside the adventure playground.
P is the same distance from A as it is from C.
P is the same distance from AC as it is from AB.
On the diagram, clearly mark the point P.

(3 marks)

2 A cuboid lies on the coordinate axes.
The point R has coordinates (5, 4, 3).
Write down the coordinates of point S.

(1 mark)

Score   / 4

How well did you do?

0–4 Try again   5–8 Getting there   9–13 Good work   14–17 Excellent!

For more information on this topic, see page 68 of your Success Revision Guide.

Angle properties of circles

Multiple-choice questions

Choose just one answer, a, b, c or d. Circle your choice.

Questions 1–5 refer to the diagrams drawn below.

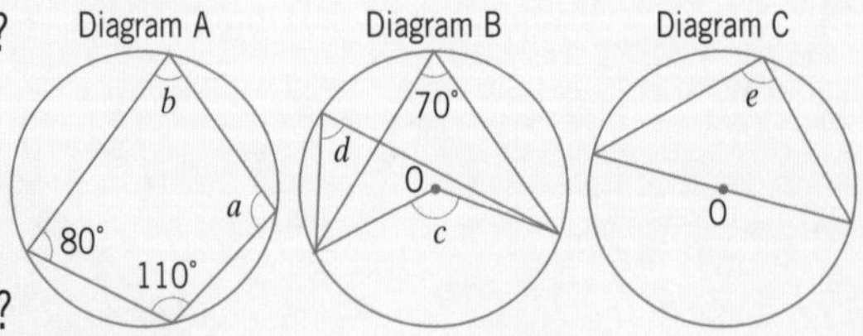

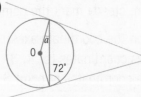

Diagram A   Diagram B   Diagram C

1 In diagram A, what is the size of angle *a*?

   a) 80°   b) 110°

   c) 100°   d) 70°   (1 mark)

2 In diagram A, what is the size of angle *b*?

   a) 70°   b) 110°   c) 100°   d) 80°   (1 mark)

3 In diagram B, what is the size of angle *c*?

   a) 35°   b) 70°   c) 100°   d) 140°   (1 mark)

4 In diagram B, what is the size of angle *d*?

   a) 70°   b) 35°   c) 100°   d) 140°   (1 mark)

5 In diagram C, what is the size of angle *e*?

   a) 100°   b) 45°   c) 90°   d) 110°   (1 mark)

Score   / 5

Short-answer questions

Answer all parts of each question.

1 Some angles are written on cards. Match the missing angle *a* in the diagrams below
with the correct card. O represents the centre of the circle.

      50° 60° 82° 65° 18°

a)

b)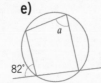

c)

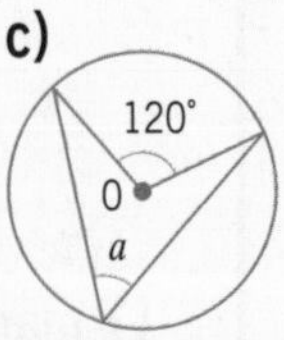

d)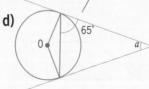

e)

(5 marks)

2 John says, 'Angle *a* is 42°.'

Explain whether John is correct.

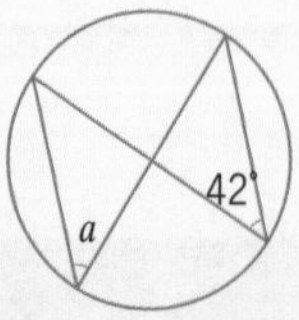

_____

_____

(1 mark)

Score   / 6

Answer all parts of the questions. Show your workings (on a separate sheet of paper if necessary) and include the correct units in your answers.

1 PQ and PR are tangents to a circle, centre O.
Point S is a point on the circumference.
Angle RSQ is 70°.

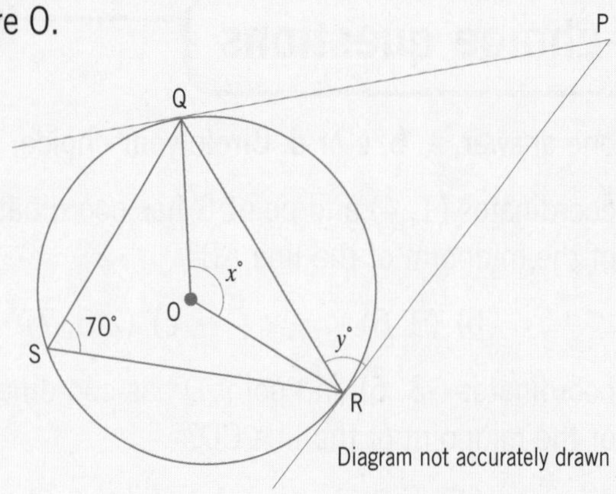

Diagram not accurately drawn

  a) Find the size of angle ROQ, marked $x°$ in the diagram.

  _____ °

  (2 marks)

  b) Find the size of angle PRQ, marked $y°$ in the diagram.

  _____ °

  (4 marks)

2 A, B and C are points on a circle, centre O. DE is a tangent to the circle at point C. Angle BCE is 71°.
Find the size of angle BAC.
Give a reason for your answer.

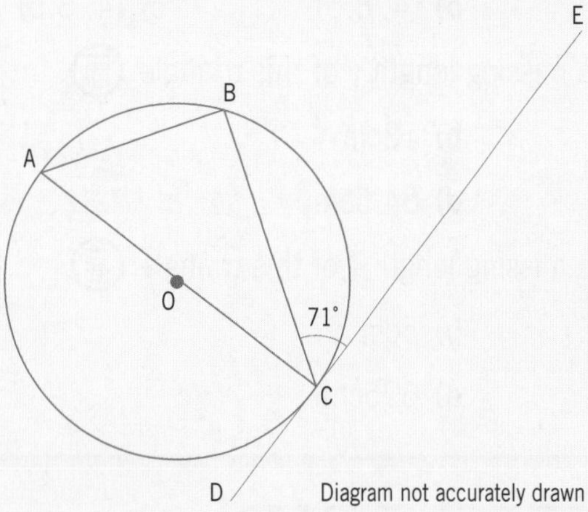

Diagram not accurately drawn

_____

_____

_____

_____

(2 marks)

3 A and B are two points on a circle, centre O. BC is a tangent to the circle.
Angle ABC = y.

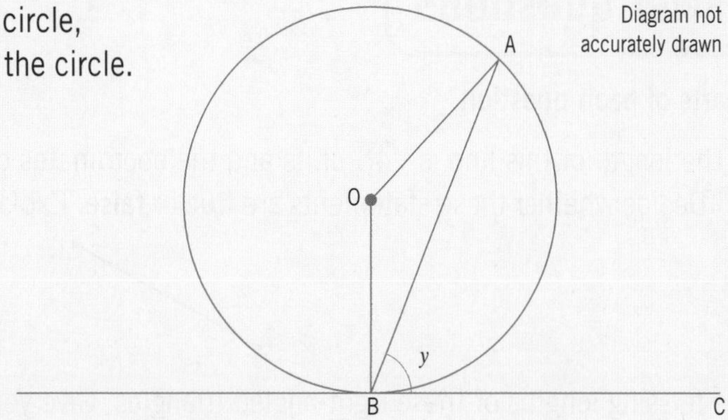

Diagram not accurately drawn

Billy says that angle AOB = $2y$. Prove whether Billy is correct. You must give reasons for each stage of your working.

_____

_____

_____

(4 marks)

Score   / 12

How well did you do?

| 0–4 | Try again | 5–9 | Getting there | 10–14 | Good work | 15–23 | Excellent! |

For more information on this topic, see page 69 of your Success Revision Guide.

Pythagoras' theorem

Multiple-choice questions

Choose just one answer, a, b, c or d. Circle your choice.

1 Point A has coordinates (1, 4) and point B has coordinates (4, 10). What are the coordinates of the midpoint of the line AB?

    a) (5, 14)   **b)** (3, 6)   **c)** (2.5, 7)   **d)** (1.5, 3)   (1 mark)

2 Point C has coordinates (-3, 5) and point D has coordinates (5, 12). What are the coordinates of the midpoint of the line CD?

    a) (1, 3.5)   **b)** (4, 8.5)   **c)** (4, 3.5)   **d)** (1, 8.5)   (1 mark)

3 Calculate the missing length y of this triangle.

    a) 169cm   **b)** 13cm

    c) 17cm   **d)** 84.5cm   (1 mark)

12cm, y, 5cm

4 Calculate the missing length y of this triangle.

    a) 13.2cm   **b)** 5cm

    c) 25cm   **d)** 625cm   (1 mark)

20cm, y, 15cm

Score   / 4

Short-answer questions

Answer all parts of each question.

1 Colin says, 'The length of this line is $\sqrt{45}$ units and the coordinates of the midpoint are (3.5, 8).' Decide whether these statements are **true** or **false**. Explain your answer.

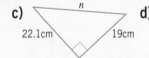

(5, 11)

(2, 5)

    (2 marks)

2 Calculate the missing lengths of these right-angled triangles. Give your answer to 3 significant figures, where appropriate.

    a)   **b)**   **c)**   **d)**

    12cm, n, 9cm   *n, 15.2cm, 8.5cm*   *n, 22.1cm, 19cm*   *31cm, n, 18.9cm*

    $n =$ _____ cm $n =$ _____ cm $n =$ _____ cm $n =$ _____ cm   (8 marks)

3 Molly says, 'The angle $x°$ in this triangle is 90°.' Explain how Molly knows this without measuring the size of the angle.

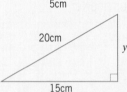

12cm, 13cm, $x°$, 5cm

    (2 marks)

Score   / 12

Answer all parts of the questions. Show your workings (on a separate sheet of paper if necessary) and include the correct units in your answers.

1 Calculate the perpendicular height of this isosceles triangle.
Give your answer to 1 decimal place. 🖩

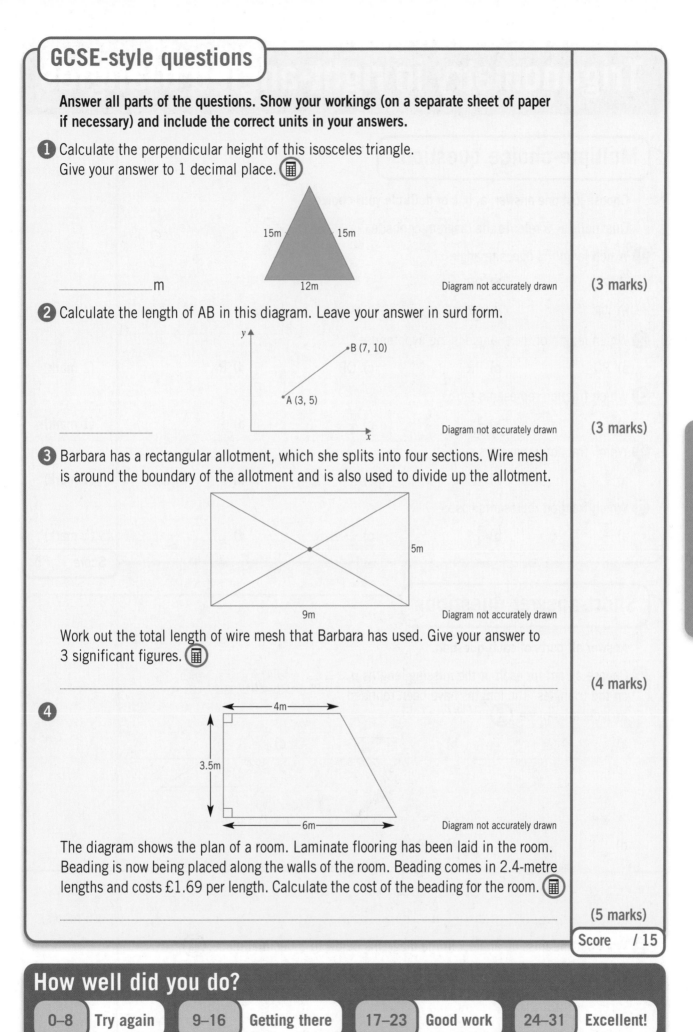

_____ m   15m   15m   12m   Diagram not accurately drawn   **(3 marks)**

2 Calculate the length of AB in this diagram. Leave your answer in surd form.

B (7, 10)

A (3, 5)

Diagram not accurately drawn   **(3 marks)**

_____

3 Barbara has a rectangular allotment, which she splits into four sections. Wire mesh is around the boundary of the allotment and is also used to divide up the allotment.

5m

9m   Diagram not accurately drawn

Work out the total length of wire mesh that Barbara has used. Give your answer to 3 significant figures. 🖩

_____

(4 marks)

4

4m

3.5m

6m   Diagram not accurately drawn

The diagram shows the plan of a room. Laminate flooring has been laid in the room. Beading is now being placed along the walls of the room. Beading comes in 2.4-metre lengths and costs £1.69 per length. Calculate the cost of the beading for the room. 🖩

(5 marks)

Score   / 15

How well did you do?

| 0–8 | Try again | 9–16 | Getting there | 17–23 | Good work | 24–31 | Excellent! |

For more information on this topic, see pages 70–71 of your Success Revision Guide.

Geometry and measures

Trigonometry in right-angled triangles

Multiple-choice questions

Choose just one answer, a, b, c or d. Circle your choice.

Questions 1–5 refer to the diagram opposite.

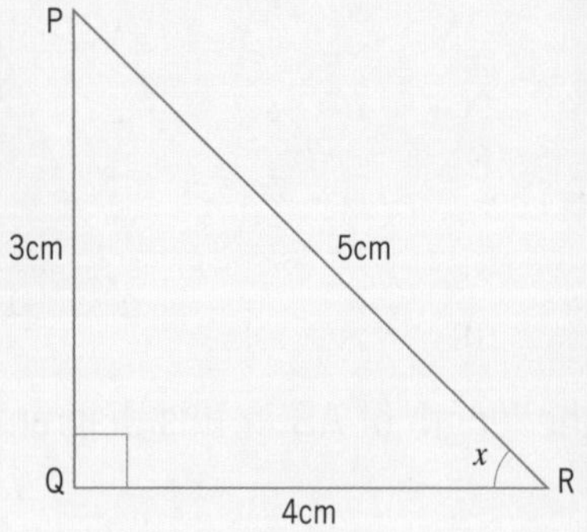

1 Which length is opposite angle x?

a) PQ   b) PR

c) QR   d) RX   (1 mark)

2 Which length of the triangle is the hypotenuse?

a) PQ   b) PR   c) QR   d) RX   (1 mark)

3 Which fraction represents tan x?

a) $\frac{3}{5}$ b) $\frac{4}{3}$ c) $\frac{4}{5}$ d) $\frac{3}{4}$ (1 mark)

4 Which fraction represents sin x?

a) $\frac{3}{5}$ b) $\frac{4}{3}$ c) $\frac{5}{3}$ d) $\frac{4}{5}$ (1 mark)

5 Which fraction represents cos x?

a) $\frac{3}{5}$ b) $\frac{3}{4}$ c) $\frac{4}{5}$ d) $\frac{5}{4}$ (1 mark)

Score   / 5

Short-answer questions

Answer all parts of each question.

1 Choose a card for each of the missing lengths n on the triangles. The lengths have been rounded to 1 decimal place.

a)

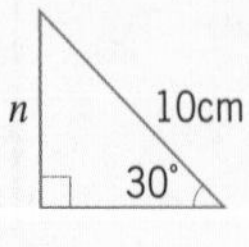

$n = $ _____

b)

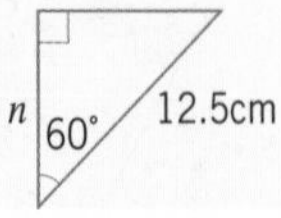

$n = $ _____

c)

$n = $ _____

d)

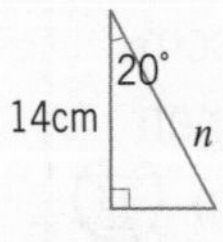

$n = $ _____

e)

$n = $ _____   (5 marks)

2 Work out the missing angle x in the diagrams below to 1 decimal place.

a)

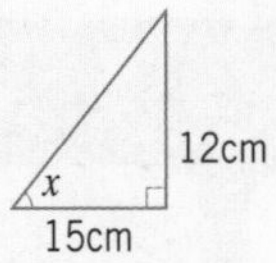

$x = $ _____ °

b)

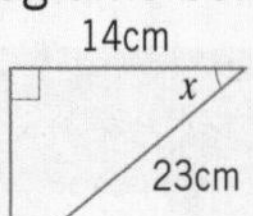

$x = $ _____ °

c)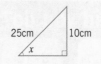

$x = $ _____ °   (6 marks)

Score   / 11

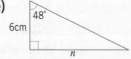

Geometry and measures

58

Answer all parts of the questions. Show your workings (on a separate sheet of paper if necessary) and include the correct units in your answers.

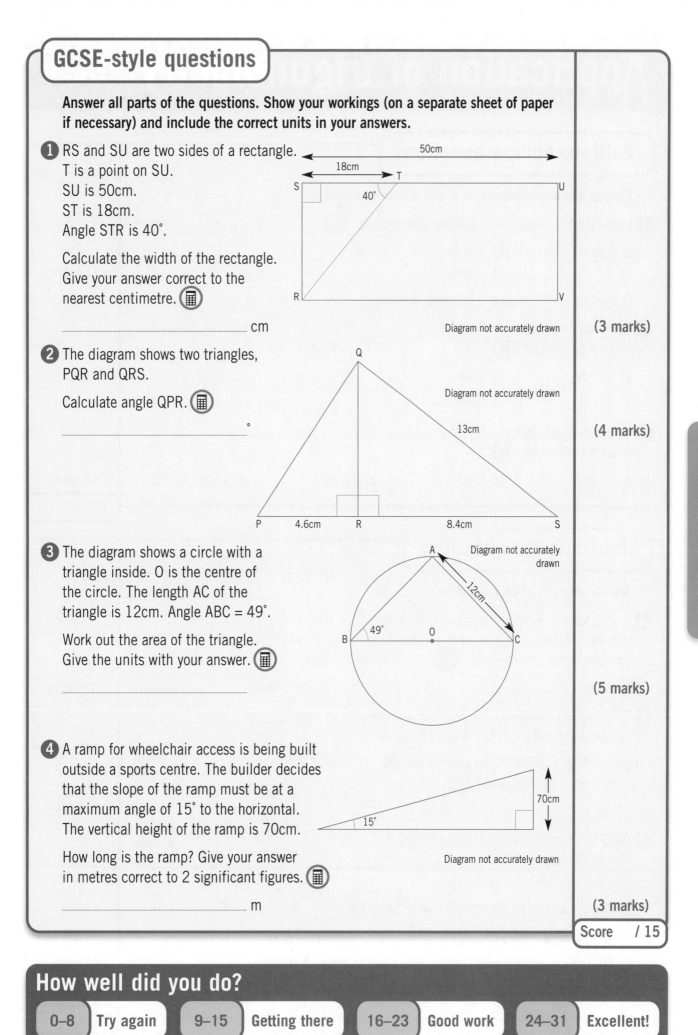

1 RS and SU are two sides of a rectangle.
T is a point on SU.
SU is 50cm.
ST is 18cm.
Angle STR is 40°.

Calculate the width of the rectangle.
Give your answer correct to the
nearest centimetre. 🖩

_____ cm

Diagram not accurately drawn

(3 marks)

2 The diagram shows two triangles,
PQR and QRS.

Calculate angle QPR. 🖩

_____ °

Diagram not accurately drawn

(4 marks)

3 The diagram shows a circle with a
triangle inside. O is the centre of
the circle. The length AC of the
triangle is 12cm. Angle ABC = 49°.

Work out the area of the triangle.
Give the units with your answer. 🖩

_____

Diagram not accurately drawn

(5 marks)

4 A ramp for wheelchair access is being built
outside a sports centre. The builder decides
that the slope of the ramp must be at a
maximum angle of 15° to the horizontal.
The vertical height of the ramp is 70cm.

How long is the ramp? Give your answer
in metres correct to 2 significant figures. 🖩

_____ m

Diagram not accurately drawn

(3 marks)

Score   / 15

How well did you do?

| 0–8 | **Try again** | 9–15 | **Getting there** | 16–23 | **Good work** | 24–31 | **Excellent!** |

For more information on this topic, see pages 69 and 72–73 of your Success Revision Guide.

59

Application of trigonometry

Multiple-choice questions

Choose just one answer, a, b, c or d. Circle your choice.

1️⃣ Calculate the value of x in the triangle opposite. 🖩

   a) 13cm   **b)** 8.7cm

   c) 7.5cm   **d)** 10cm   **(1 mark)**

Questions 2–3 refer to the following cuboid.

2️⃣ Calculate the length of AC to the nearest centimetre. 🖩

   a) 13cm   **b)** 11cm

   c) 12cm   **d)** 14cm   **(1 mark)**

3️⃣ Calculate the length of AD to the nearest centimetre. 🖩

   a) 11cm   **b)** 13cm   **c)** 12cm   **d)** 14cm   **(1 mark)**

Diagram not accurately drawn

Score   / 3

Short-answer questions

Answer all parts of each question.

1️⃣ A ship sails 20km due north and then 50km due east. What is the bearing of the finishing point from the starting point? 🖩

   Bearing = _____ °   **(2 marks)**

2️⃣ The diagram represents the sector of a circle with centre O and radius 12cm. Angle POR = 70°.

   Calculate the length of the straight line PR, correct to 1 decimal place. 🖩

   _____ cm   **(3 marks)**

3️⃣ CDEFGH is a right-angled triangular prism. N is the midpoint of DE.

   a) Are the following statements **true** or **false**? 🖩

      i) The length HD is 19.2cm, correct to 3 significant figures. _____   **(1 mark)**

      ii) The size of angle HDC is 51.3°, correct to 1 decimal place. _____   **(1 mark)**

   b) Calculate the size of angle HNC, correct to 1 decimal place. 🖩 _____ °   **(3 marks)**

Score   / 10

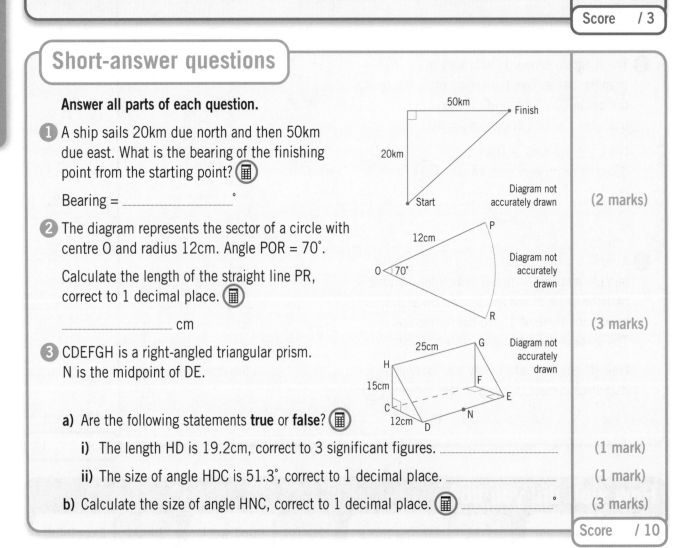

60

GCSE-style questions

Answer all parts of the questions. Show your workings (on a separate sheet of paper if necessary) and include the correct units in your answers.

1 The diagram shows a triangle PQR.
PS = 6.5cm, QR = 12.7cm and angle QRS = 62°.
Calculate the size of the angle marked x°.
Give your answer correct to 1 decimal place. 🔢

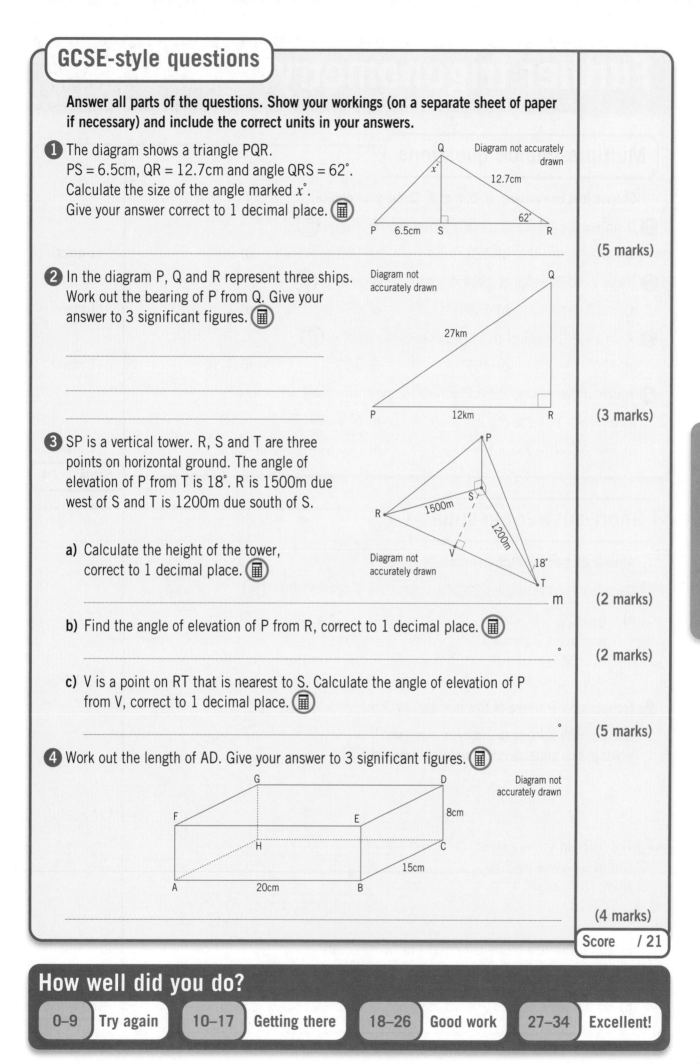

Diagram not accurately drawn

(5 marks)

2 In the diagram P, Q and R represent three ships.
Work out the bearing of P from Q. Give your answer to 3 significant figures. 🔢

Diagram not accurately drawn

(3 marks)

3 SP is a vertical tower. R, S and T are three points on horizontal ground. The angle of elevation of P from T is 18°. R is 1500m due west of S and T is 1200m due south of S.

Diagram not accurately drawn

a) Calculate the height of the tower, correct to 1 decimal place. 🔢

_____ m

(2 marks)

b) Find the angle of elevation of P from R, correct to 1 decimal place. 🔢

_____ °

(2 marks)

c) V is a point on RT that is nearest to S. Calculate the angle of elevation of P from V, correct to 1 decimal place. 🔢

_____ °

(5 marks)

4 Work out the length of AD. Give your answer to 3 significant figures. 🔢

Diagram not accurately drawn

(4 marks)

Score   / 21

How well did you do?

| 0–9 | Try again | 10–17 | Getting there | 18–26 | Good work | 27–34 | Excellent! |

For more information on this topic, see pages 72–75 of your Success Revision Guide.

Further trigonometry

Geometry and measures

Multiple-choice questions

Choose just one answer, a, b, c or d. Circle your choice.

1 If $\sin x = 0.5$, which of these is a possible value of x?

   a) 180°   **b)** 120°   **c)** 150°   **d)** 90°   (1 mark)

2 If $\cos x = 0.5$, which of these is a possible value of x?

   a) 300°   **b)** 150°   **c)** 65°   **d)** 120°   (1 mark)

3 If $\sin x = \frac{\sqrt{3}}{2}$, which of these is a possible value of x?

   a) 320°   **b)** 400°   **c)** 360°   **d)** 420°   (1 mark)

4 Which of these is the correct formula for the cosine rule?

   a) $a^2 = b^2 - c^2 + 2bc \cos A$ **b)** $b^2 = a^2 + c^2 - 2bc \cos B$

   c) $a^2 = b^2 + c^2 - 2bc \cos A$ **d)** $c^2 = b^2 + a^2 - 2ab \cos A$ (1 mark)

Score   / 4

Short-answer questions

Answer all parts of each question.

1 Calculate the missing lengths or angles in the diagrams below.

Diagrams not accurately drawn

a)

b)

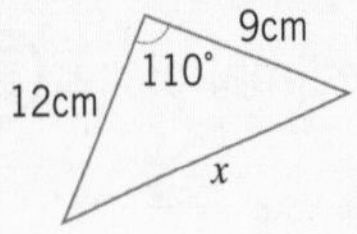

c)

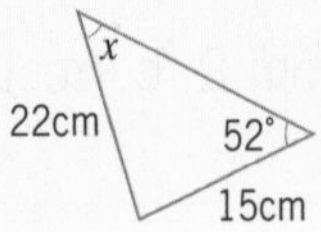

d)

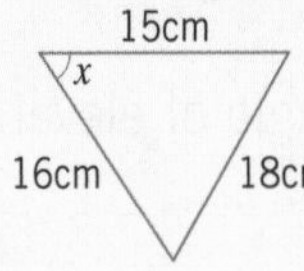

$x = $ _____cm $x = $ _____cm $x = $ _____° $x = $ _____°   (8 marks)

2 Isobel says, 'The area of this triangle is 70cm².'

Decide, with working to justify your answer, whether this statement is **correct** or **incorrect**.

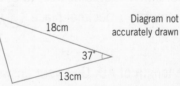

Diagram not accurately drawn

_____

_____   (2 marks)

3 The diagram shows a sketch of part of the curve $y = f(x)$, where $f(x) = \cos x°$.

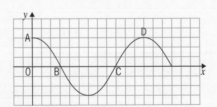

a) Write down the coordinates of the following points.

   A (_____ , _____)   B (_____ , _____)   C (_____ , _____)   D (_____ , _____)   (4 marks)

b) On the same diagram, sketch the graph of $y = \cos 2x$.   (3 marks)

Score   / 17

Answer all parts of the questions. Show your workings (on a separate sheet of paper if necessary) and include the correct units in your answers.

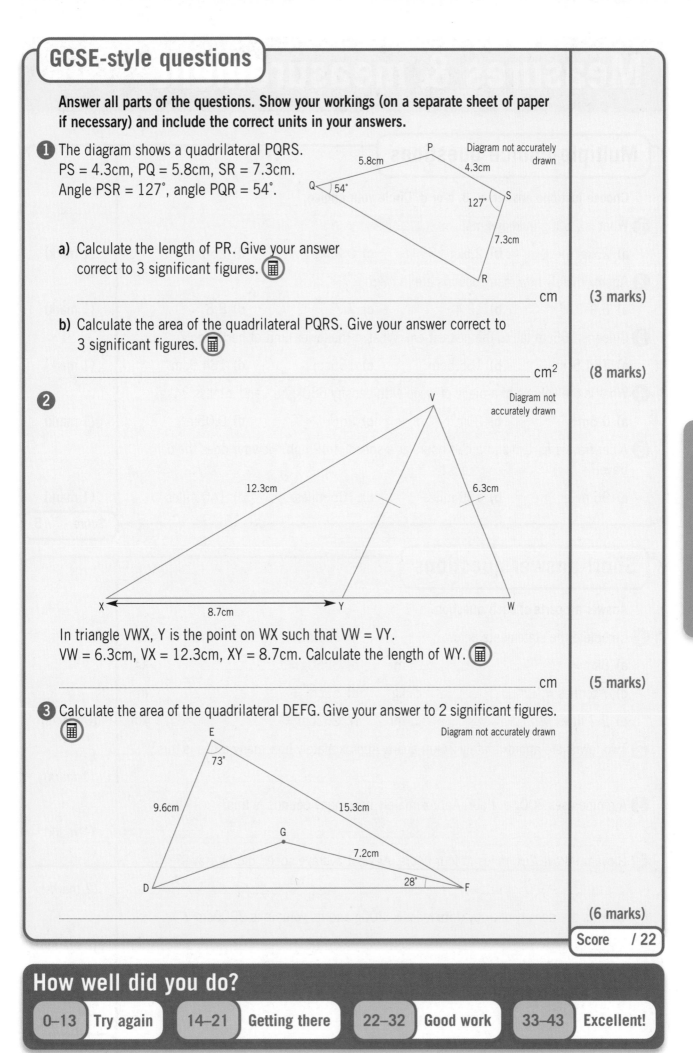

1 The diagram shows a quadrilateral PQRS.
PS = 4.3cm, PQ = 5.8cm, SR = 7.3cm.
Angle PSR = 127°, angle PQR = 54°.

5.8cm P Diagram not accurately drawn
4.3cm
Q 54°
127° S
7.3cm
R

   a) Calculate the length of PR. Give your answer
      correct to 3 significant figures. 🖩

   _____ cm   (3 marks)

   b) Calculate the area of the quadrilateral PQRS. Give your answer correct to
      3 significant figures. 🖩

   _____ cm²   (8 marks)

2

V Diagram not accurately drawn

12.3cm   6.3cm

X ◄————————► Y   W
       8.7cm

In triangle VWX, Y is the point on WX such that VW = VY.
VW = 6.3cm, VX = 12.3cm, XY = 8.7cm. Calculate the length of WY. 🖩

   _____ cm   (5 marks)

3 Calculate the area of the quadrilateral DEFG. Give your answer to 2 significant figures.
🖩

E   Diagram not accurately drawn
73°

9.6cm   15.3cm

       G
          7.2cm
D   28° F

                                                                    (6 marks)

Score   / 22

How well did you do?

0–13 Try again   14–21 Getting there   22–32 Good work   33–43 Excellent!

For more information on this topic, see pages 76–77 of your Success Revision Guide.

Geometry and measures

63

Measures & measurement

Multiple-choice questions

Choose just one answer, a, b, c or d. Circle your choice.

1 What is 2500g in kilograms?

   a) 25kg   **b)** 2.5kg   **c)** 0.25kg   **d)** 250kg   **(1 mark)**

2 Approximately how many pounds are in 4kg?

   a) 6.9   **b)** 12.4   **c)** 7.7   **d)** 8.8   **(1 mark)**

3 Chloe is 165cm tall to the nearest cm. What is the lower limit of her height?

   a) 164.5cm   **b)** 165.5cm   **c)** 165cm   **d)** 164.9cm   **(1 mark)**

4 What is the volume of a piece of wood with density 680kg/m^{-3} and a mass 34kg?

   a) 0.5m^3 **b)** 20m^3 **c)** 2m^3 **d)** 0.05m^3 **(1 mark)**

5 A car travels for two and a half hours at a speed of 42mph. How far does the car travel?

   a) 96 miles   **b)** 100 miles   **c)** 105 miles   **d)** 140 miles   **(1 mark)**

Score   / 5

Short-answer questions

Answer all parts of each question.

1 Complete the statements below.

   a) 8km = _____ m   **b)** 3250g = _____ kg

   c) 7 tonnes = _____ kg   **d)** 52cm = _____ m

   e) 2.7 litres = _____ ml   **f)** 262cm = _____ km   **(6 marks)**

2 Two towns are approximately 24km apart. Approximately how many miles is this?

   (1 mark)

3 A recipe uses 500g of flour. Approximately how many pounds is this?

   (1 mark)

4 Giovanni drove 200 miles in four hours. At what average speed did he travel?

   (2 marks)

5 What is the density of a toy if its mass is 200g and its volume is 2000cm^3?

   (2 marks)

6 A field is 47 metres long to the nearest metre. Write down the upper and lower limits of the length of the field.

   (2 marks)

Score   / 14

GCSE-style questions

Answer all parts of the questions. Show your workings (on a separate sheet of paper if necessary) and include the correct units in your answers.

1 a) Change 8 kilograms into pounds. _____ pounds   (2 marks)

   b) Change 30 miles into kilometres. _____ km   (2 marks)

2 The length of the rectangle is 12.1cm to the nearest mm. The width of the rectangle is 6cm to the nearest cm. Write down the lower limits for the length and width of the rectangle.

12.1cm

6cm

Length _____ cm

Width _____ cm   (2 marks)

3 Amy took part in a sponsored walk. She walked from the school to the park and back. The distance from the school to the park is 8km.

   a) Amy walked from the school to the park at an average speed of 5km/h. Find the time she took to walk from the school to the park. 🖩

   _____   (2 marks)

   b) Her average speed for the return journey was 4km/h. Calculate her average speed for the whole journey. 🖩

   _____   (4 marks)

4 Two solids each have a volume of $2.5m^3$.
The density of solid A is 320kg per m^3.
The density of solid B is 288kg per m^3.

A   B

Calculate the difference in the masses of the solids. 🖩

_____ kg   (3 marks)

5 The speed limit through some roadworks is 50mph. Cameras recorded the time taken for a car to travel 2400m through the roadworks as 108 seconds. 10mph is approximately 4.47m/s. Was the car speeding through the roadworks? You must show your working. 🖩

_____

_____   (5 marks)

Score   / 20

How well did you do?

| 0–13 | Try again | 14–22 | Getting there | 23–31 | Good work | 32–39 | Excellent! |

For more information on this topic, see pages 78–79 of your *Success Revision Guide*.

Geometry and measures

65

Area of 2D shapes

Multiple-choice questions

Choose just one answer, a, b, c or d. Circle your choice.

1 What is the area of this triangle?

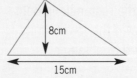

a) 60mm²   b) 120cm²

c) 60cm²   d) 46cm²

(1 mark)

2 If the area of a rectangle is 20cm² and its width is 2.5cm, what is its length?

a) 9cm   b) 8cm   c) 7.5cm   d) 2.5cm

(1 mark)

3 What is the area of this circle? Use π = 3.142 🖩

a) 25.1cm²   b) 55cm²

c) 12.6cm²   d) 50.3cm²

(1 mark)

4 What is the approximate circumference of a circle of radius 4cm? 🖩

a) 25.1cm²   b) 50.3cm   c) 12.6cm   d) 25.1cm

(1 mark)

Score / 4

Short-answer questions

Answer all parts of each question.

1 For each of the diagrams below, state whether the area given is **true** or **false**.

a)
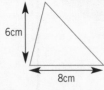

Area = 48cm²

b)
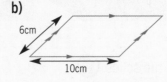

Area = 60cm²

c)
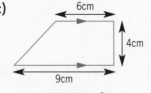

Area = 108cm²

(3 marks)

2 Calculate the area of the region shaded green.

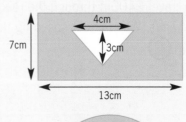

_____ cm²

(3 marks)

3 Calculate the perimeter of this shape, correct to 1 decimal place. Use the π button on your calculator or π = 3.142 🖩

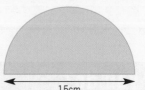

_____ cm

(3 marks)

4 Change 7m² to cm². _____

(2 marks)

Score / 11

GCSE-style questions

Answer all parts of the questions. Show your workings (on a separate sheet of paper if necessary) and include the correct units in your answers.

1 The diagram opposite shows the plan of a garden. Lawn seed is to be sown to cover the garden. Lawn seed comes in 500g packets and covers $14m^2$. A packet of lawn seed costs £5.50. Work out the total cost of the lawn seed needed.

(5 marks)

2 The diagram opposite shows the plan of a room. Underfloor heating is being installed in the room. $1m^2$ of underfloor heating costs £155. Work out the total cost of installing underfloor heating for the whole room.

(5 marks)

3 The diagram opposite shows the plan of a running track. Work out the total distance of the running track. Use the π button on your calculator. Give your answer to 3 significant figures. 🖩

(3 marks)

4 The area of a circular sewing pattern is $200cm^2$. Calculate the diameter of the sewing pattern. Use the π button on your calculator. Give your answer correct to the nearest centimetre. 🖩

(4 marks)

Score   / 17

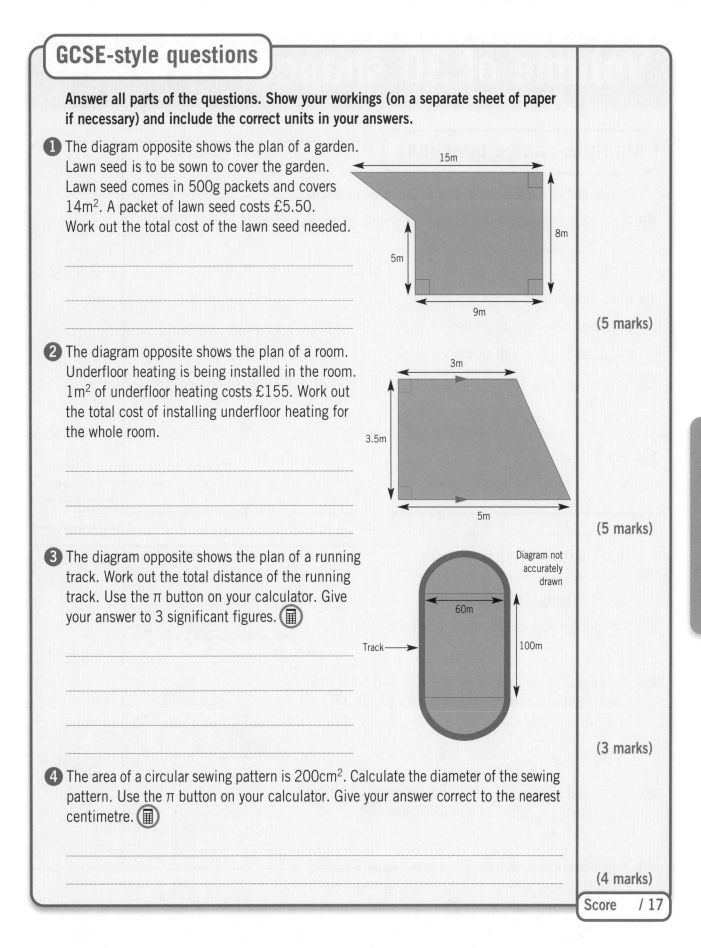

How well did you do?

| 0–8 | Try again | 9–16 | Getting there | 17–24 | Good work | 25–32 | Excellent! |

For more information on this topic, see pages 80–81 of your Success Revision Guide.

Volume of 3D shapes

Multiple-choice questions

Choose just one answer, a, b, c or d. Circle your choice.

1 The volume of a cuboid is 20cm³. If its height is 1cm and its width is 4cm, what is its length?

   a) 5cm   **b)** 10cm   **c)** 15cm   **d)** 8cm   **(1 mark)**

2 What is the volume of this prism?

   a) 64cm³   **b)** 240cm³

   c) 120cm³   **d)** 20cm³   **(1 mark)**

3 A cube of volume 2cm³ is enlarged by a scale factor of 3. What is the volume of the enlarged cube?

   a) 6cm³   **b)** 27cm³   **c)** 54cm³   **d)** 18cm³   **(1 mark)**

4 What is 5m³ in cm³?

   a) 500cm³   **b)** 5000cm³   **c)** 500 000cm³   **d)** 5 000 000cm³   **(1 mark)**

Score   / 4

Short-answer questions

Answer all parts of each question.

1 Work out the surface area of the triangular prism.

   _____ cm²   **(4 marks)**

2 Emily says, 'The volume of this prism is 345.6m³.' Is Emily correct? Show working out to justify your answer.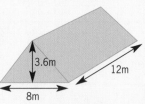

   _____

   _____   **(1 mark)**

3 Calculate the volume of this cylinder, clearly stating your units. Use the π button on your calculator.

   _____   **(2 marks)**

4 If the volume of both these solids is the same, work out the height of the cylinder to 1 decimal place. Use the π button on your calculator.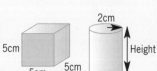

   _____ cm   **(4 marks)**

5 The volume of a cube is 141cm³. Each length of the cube is enlarged by a scale factor of 3. What is the volume of the enlarged cube?

   _____ cm³   **(2 marks)**

Score   / 13

Answer all parts of the questions. Show your workings (on a separate sheet of paper if necessary) and include the correct units in your answers.

1 A cube has a surface area of 96cm^2. Work out the volume of the cube.

_____ cm^3 **(4 marks)**

2 A metal door wedge is in the shape of a prism with cross-section VWXY.
VW = 7cm, VY = 15cm, WX = 9cm.
The width of the door wedge is 0.08m.

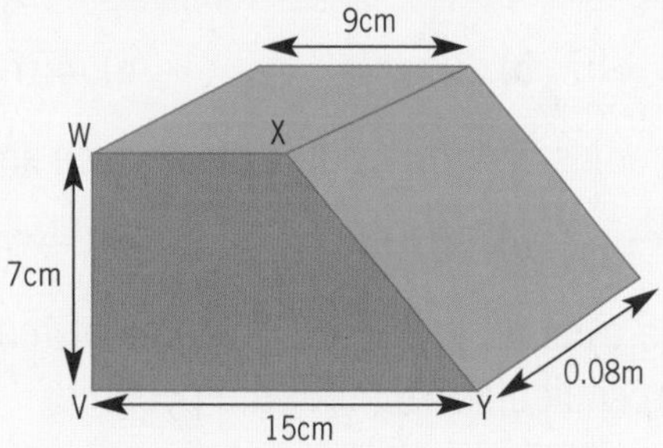

a) Calculate the volume of the door wedge in cm^3. 🖩

_____ cm^3 **(3 marks)**

b) The density of the metal is 5.5 grams per cm^3.
Work out the mass of the door wedge. 🖩

_____ g   **(2 marks)**

3 Albert wants to paint the outside walls, roof and door of his shed (shown opposite) with wood preservative. The shed does not have any windows. A tin of wood preservative covers 20m^2. Each tin costs £8.45. Work out how much it will cost Albert to paint all four walls, the roof and door of his shed. 🖩

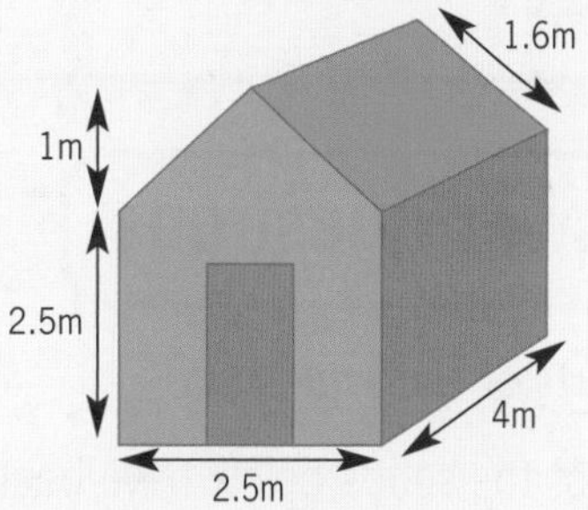

_____   **(6 marks)**

4 The volume of this cylinder is 250cm^3.
The height of the cylinder is 8cm.

Calculate the radius of the cylinder, giving your answer to 1 decimal place. Use π = 3.142 🖩

_____ cm   **(3 marks)**

Score   / 18

Geometry and measures

How well did you do?

| 0–9 | Try again | 10–18 | Getting there | 19–27 | Good work | 28–35 | Excellent! |

For more information on this topic, see pages 67 and 82–83 of your Success Revision Guide.

69

Further length, area & volume

Multiple-choice questions

Choose just one answer, a, b, c or d. Circle your choice.

1 A sphere has a radius of 3cm. What is the volume of the sphere given in terms of π?

  a) 12π   **b)** 36π   **c)** 42π   **d)** $\frac{81}{4}$ π   **(1 mark)**

2 A sphere has a radius of 4cm. What is the surface area of the sphere given in terms of π?

  a) 64π   **b)** 32π   **c)** $\frac{256}{3}$ π   **d)** 25π   **(1 mark)**

3 The volume of a pyramid is 25cm³. The area of the base is 12cm².
What is the perpendicular height of the pyramid?

  a) 7.2cm   **b)** 4cm   **c)** 25cm   **d)** 6.25cm   **(1 mark)**

Questions 4–5 refer to the circle diagram opposite.

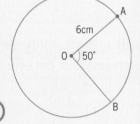

4 What is the length of the minor arc AOB? Use the π button.

  a) 5.2cm   **b)** 5.8cm

  c) 6.2cm   **d)** 7.4cm   **(1 mark)**

5 What is the area of the minor sector AOB? Use the π button.

  a) 15.2cm²   **b)** 25.3cm²   **c)** 15.7cm²   **d)** 16.9cm²   **(1 mark)**

Score   / 5

Short-answer questions

Answer all parts of each question.

1 The volumes of the solids below have been calculated. Match each solid with its correct volume. Use the π button on your calculator.

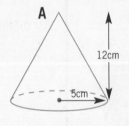
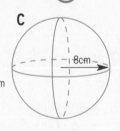
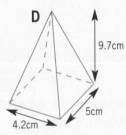

      600cm³ _____   68cm³ _____   314cm³ _____   2145cm³ _____   **(8 marks)**

2 State whether this statement is **true** or **false**. You must show sufficient working in order to justify your answer.

'The area of the shaded segment is 3.26cm².'

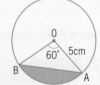

_____

_____

(3 marks)

Score   / 11

GCSE-style questions

Answer all parts of the questions. Show your workings (on a separate sheet of paper if necessary) and include the correct units in your answers.

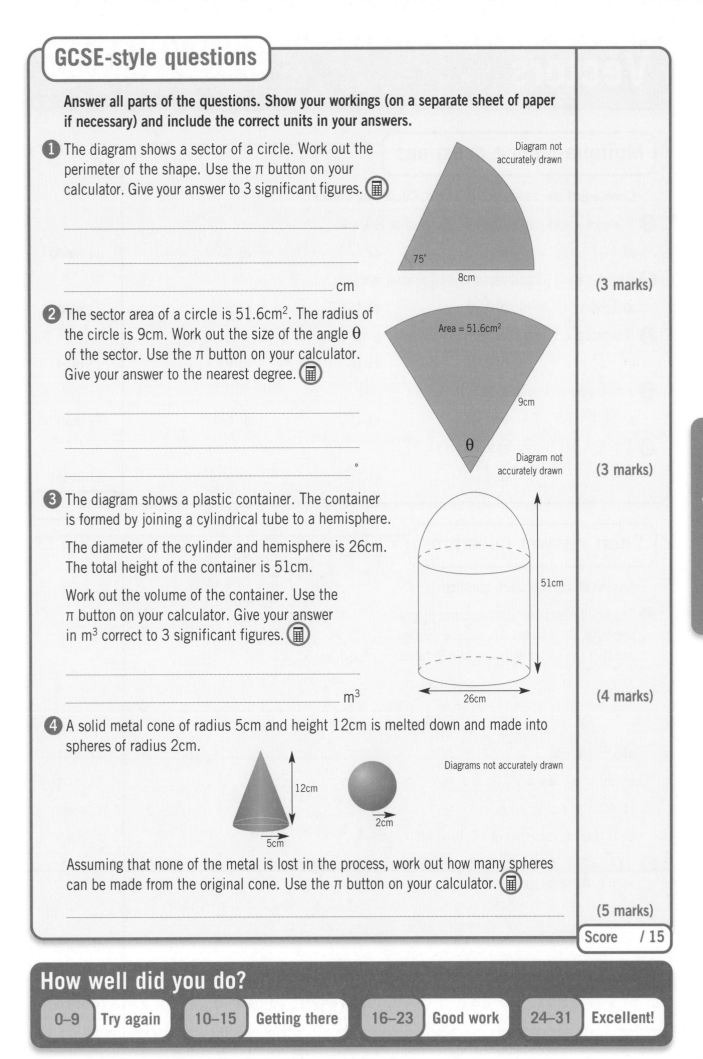

1 The diagram shows a sector of a circle. Work out the perimeter of the shape. Use the π button on your calculator. Give your answer to 3 significant figures. 🖩

Diagram not accurately drawn

75°

8cm

_____ cm

(3 marks)

2 The sector area of a circle is 51.6cm². The radius of the circle is 9cm. Work out the size of the angle θ of the sector. Use the π button on your calculator. Give your answer to the nearest degree. 🖩

Area = 51.6cm²

9cm

θ

Diagram not accurately drawn

_____ °

(3 marks)

3 The diagram shows a plastic container. The container is formed by joining a cylindrical tube to a hemisphere.

The diameter of the cylinder and hemisphere is 26cm. The total height of the container is 51cm.

Work out the volume of the container. Use the π button on your calculator. Give your answer in m³ correct to 3 significant figures. 🖩

51cm

26cm

_____ m³

(4 marks)

4 A solid metal cone of radius 5cm and height 12cm is melted down and made into spheres of radius 2cm.

Diagrams not accurately drawn

12cm

5cm

2cm

Assuming that none of the metal is lost in the process, work out how many spheres can be made from the original cone. Use the π button on your calculator. 🖩

(5 marks)

Score   / 15

How well did you do?

| 0–9 | Try again | 10–15 | Getting there | 16–23 | Good work | 24–31 | Excellent! |

For more information on this topic, see pages 84–85 of your Success Revision Guide.

71

Vectors

Multiple-choice questions

Choose just one answer, a, b, c or d. Circle your choice.

1 If vector $\mathbf{a} = \binom{2}{3}$ and vector $\mathbf{b} = \binom{-5}{-2}$, what is $\mathbf{a} + \mathbf{b}$?

     a) $\binom{1}{-3}$ b) $\binom{-3}{1}$ c) $\binom{7}{-5}$ d) $\binom{-10}{-6}$ **(1 mark)**

2 If vector $\mathbf{c} = \binom{-4}{2}$ and vector $\mathbf{d} = \binom{-6}{-5}$, what is $\mathbf{c} - \mathbf{d}$?

     a) $\binom{8}{-14}$ b) $\binom{-6}{-5}$ c) $\binom{2}{7}$ d) $\binom{-6}{5}$ **(1 mark)**

3 If vector $\mathbf{p} = \binom{7}{-2}$ and vector $\mathbf{r} = \binom{-9}{2}$, what is $4\mathbf{p} + \mathbf{r}$?

     a) $\binom{19}{-6}$ b) $\binom{38}{0}$ c) $\binom{-6}{19}$ d) $\binom{20}{-3}$ **(1 mark)**

4 Which vector is parallel to $\binom{2}{5}$?

     a) $\binom{10}{20}$ b) $\binom{6}{15}$ c) $\binom{20}{45}$ d) $\binom{1}{2}$ **(1 mark)**

5 Which vector is parallel to vector $\mathbf{r} = \binom{-4}{6}$?

     a) $\binom{-8}{6}$ b) $\binom{-16}{24}$ c) $\binom{-4}{12}$ d) $\binom{-8}{18}$ **(1 mark)**

Score   / 5

Short-answer questions

Answer all parts of each question.

1 The statements below refer to the diagram opposite. $\overrightarrow{OA} = \mathbf{a}$, $\overrightarrow{AB} = \mathbf{b}$, $\overrightarrow{OC} = \mathbf{c}$. State whether the statements are **true** or **false**.

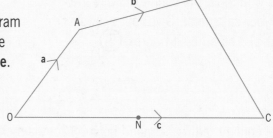

   a) $\overrightarrow{OB} = \mathbf{a} + \mathbf{b}$ **(1 mark)**

   b) $\overrightarrow{BC} = -\mathbf{a} + \mathbf{b} + \mathbf{c}$ **(1 mark)**

   c) $\overrightarrow{AC} = -\mathbf{a} + \mathbf{c}$ **(1 mark)**

   d) If N is the midpoint of OC, then $\overrightarrow{AN} = -\frac{1}{2}\mathbf{c} + \mathbf{a}$ **(1 mark)**

2 If $\overrightarrow{OC} = 2\mathbf{a} - 3\mathbf{b}$ and $\overrightarrow{OD} = 12\mathbf{a} - 18\mathbf{b}$, write down two geometrical facts about the vectors $\overrightarrow{OC}$ and $\overrightarrow{OD}$.

         (2 marks)

3 On squared paper, draw the vectors **a** and **b**, then complete the statements.

   a) $\mathbf{a} = \binom{3}{2}$, $\mathbf{b} = \binom{-4}{6}$, $\mathbf{a} + \mathbf{b} = (\quad)$ **b)** $\mathbf{a} = \binom{1}{4}$, $\mathbf{b} = \binom{-2}{5}$, $\mathbf{a} - \mathbf{b} = (\quad)$ **(4 marks)**

Score   / 10

Answer all parts of the questions. Show your workings (on a separate sheet of paper if necessary) and include the correct units in your answers.

1 The diagram is a sketch.
A is the point (4, 3).
B is the point (6, 7).
Write down the vector $\overrightarrow{AB}$ as a column vector $\binom{x}{y}$.

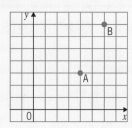

(2 marks)

2

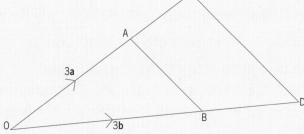

$\overrightarrow{OA}$ = 3**a**, $\overrightarrow{OB}$ = 3**b**, $\overrightarrow{OC}$ = 5**a**, $\overrightarrow{BD}$ = 2**b**. Prove that AB is parallel to CD.

(3 marks)

3

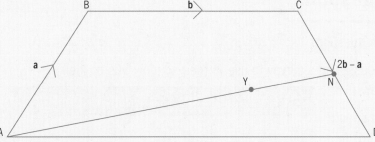

ABCD is a quadrilateral with $\overrightarrow{AB}$ = **a**, $\overrightarrow{BC}$ = **b** and $\overrightarrow{CD}$ = 2**b** – **a**.

a) Express $\overrightarrow{AC}$ in terms of **a** and **b**.   (1 mark)

b) Prove that BC is parallel to AD.

(2 marks)

c) N is the midpoint of CD. Express $\overrightarrow{AN}$ in terms of **a** and **b**.

(2 marks)

d) Y is the point on AN such that AY : YN = 3 : 1. Show that $\overrightarrow{YD} = \frac{3}{8}(4\mathbf{b} - \mathbf{a})$.

(3 marks)

Score   / 13

How well did you do?

| 0–6 | Try again | 7–12 | Getting there | 13–20 | Good work | 21–28 | Excellent! |

For more information on this topic, see pages 86–87 of your Success Revision Guide.

Geometry and measures

Collecting data

Multiple-choice questions

Choose just one answer, a, b, c or d. Circle your choice.

1 What is the name given to data you collect yourself?

   a) Continuous   **b)** Primary   **c)** Secondary   **d)** Discrete   **(1 mark)**

2 What is the name given to data in which values merge from one category to the next?

   a) Continuous   **b)** Primary   **c)** Secondary   **d)** Discrete   **(1 mark)**

3 A survey is being carried out on the number of hours some students spend watching television. In year 7 there are 240 students, year 8 has 300 students and year 9 has 460 students. Nigel decides to use a stratified sample of 100 students. How many students should he ask from year 7?

   a) 46   **b)** 30   **c)** 48   **d)** 24   **(1 mark)**

Score   / 3

Short-answer questions

Answer all parts of each question.

1 Jim and Annabelle are designing a survey to use in their school. One of their questions is shown below.

'How much time do you spend doing homework per night?'

0–1 hr	1–2 hrs	2–3 hrs	3–4 hrs

What is the problem with this question? Rewrite the question to improve it.

....

....

....

(2 marks)

2 Laura conducts a survey of the students in her school. She decides to interview 100 students. Calculate the number of students she should choose from each year group to provide a representative sample. Complete the table below.

Year group	Number of students	Number of students in sample
7	120	
8	176	
9	160	
10	190	
11	154	

(3 marks)

Score   / 5

GCSE-style questions

Answer all parts of the questions. Show your workings (on a separate sheet of paper if necessary) and include the correct units in your answers.

1 A dentist wants to encourage her patients to have a balanced diet. The dentist has approximately 80 patients. She decides to do a survey about what type of diet her patients have.

a) The following is a question in the survey. Give a criticism of this survey question.
'Do you have a healthy diet?' Yes ☐   No ☐   Sometimes ☐   Every day ☐

_____

_____   (1 mark)

b) The dentist decides to use one of two methods to do the survey.
Method 1: Choose 50 patients at random.
Method 2: Choose all the patients whose surnames begin with the letter 'A'.
Which method will give the most reliable results? Give a reason for your choice.

_____

_____   (2 marks)

2 Robert is conducting a survey into the television habits of students at his school. One of the questions in his survey is: 'Do you watch a lot of television?' His friend Jessica tells him that it is not a very good question.
Write down two ways in which Robert could improve the question.

_____

_____   (2 marks)

3 The table shows the gender and number of students in each year group of a school.

Year group	Number of boys	Number of girls	Total
7	160	120	280
8	108	132	240
9	158	117	275
10	85	70	155
11	140	110	250

Mark is carrying out a survey about how much pocket money students are given. He decides to take a stratified sample of 150 students from the whole school. Calculate how many in the stratified sample should be... 🖩

a) students from year 8 ....

b) girls from year 11. ....   (4 marks)

Score   / 9

How well did you do?

0–4 | Try again   5–8 | Getting there   9–13 | Good work   14–17 | Excellent!

For more information on this topic, see pages 90–91 of your Success Revision Guide.

Scatter graphs & correlation

Multiple-choice questions

Choose just one answer, a, b, c or d. Circle your choice.

1 A scatter graph is drawn to show the height and weight of some students. What type of correlation is likely to be shown?

  a) Zero   **b)** Negative   **c)** Positive   **d)** Scattered   **(1 mark)**

2 A scatter graph is drawn to show the maths scores and weights of some students. What type of correlation is likely to be shown?

  a) Zero   **b)** Negative   **c)** Positive   **d)** Scattered   **(1 mark)**

3 A scatter graph is drawn to show the age of some cars and their values. What type of correlation is likely to be shown?

  a) Zero   **b)** Negative   **c)** Positive   **d)** Scattered   **(1 mark)**

Score   / 3

Short-answer questions

Answer all parts of each question.

1 Some statements have been written on cards:

  (Positive correlation)   (Negative correlation)   (No correlation)

Decide which card best describes these relationships.

  a) The outside temperature and the sales of ice lollies   ....   **(1 mark)**

  b) The outside temperature and the sales of woollen gloves   ....   **(1 mark)**

  c) The mass of a person and his/her waist measurement   ....   **(1 mark)**

  d) The height of a person and his/her IQ   ....   **(1 mark)**

2 The scatter graph shows the marks scored in mathematics and physics examinations.

  a) What type of relationship is there between the mathematics and physics scores?

  ....   **(1 mark)**

  b) Draw a line of best fit on the scatter graph.   **(1 mark)**

  c) Use your line of best fit to estimate the mathematics score that Jonathan is likely to obtain if he has a physics score of 75%.

  ....   **(1 mark)**

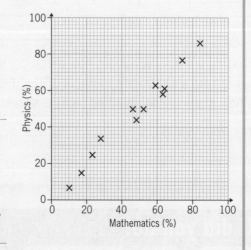

Score   / 7

Answer all parts of the questions. Show your workings (on a separate sheet of paper if necessary) and include the correct units in your answers.

1 The table shows the ages of some children and the total number of hours of sleep they had between noon on Saturday and noon on Sunday.

Age (years)	2	6	5	3	12	9	2	10	5	10	7	11	12	3
No. of hours of sleep	15	13.1	13.2	14.8	10.1	11.8	15.6	11.6	13.5	11.8	12.8	10.2	9.5	14

a) Plot the information from the table in the form of a scatter graph.

(4 marks)

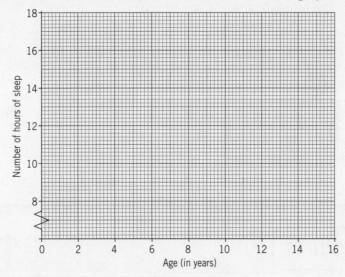

b) Describe the correlation between the age of the children and the total number of hours of sleep they had.

_____

_____

(2 marks)

c) Draw a line of best fit on your graph.

(1 mark)

d) Estimate the total number of hours of sleep for a 4-year-old child.

_____

(2 marks)

e) Explain why the line of best fit only gives an estimate for the number of hours slept.

_____

_____

(2 marks)

f) A child psychologist states, '5-year-old children have between 15 and 16 hours of sleep a night.' Decide, based on the data above, whether the child psychologist is correct.

(1 mark)

Score   / 12

How well did you do?

| 0–5 | Try again | 6–11 | Getting there | 12–16 | Good work | 17–22 | Excellent! |

For more information on this topic, see pages 94–95 of your Success Revision Guide.

Statistics and probability

Averages 1

Multiple-choice questions

Choose just one answer, a, b, c or d. Circle your choice.

1 What is the mean of this set of data? 2, 7, 1, 4, 2, 6, 2, 5, 2, 6

   a) 4.2   **b)** 3.6   **c)** 3.7   **d)** 3.9   **(1 mark)**

2 What is the median value of the set of data used in question 1?

   a) 2   **b)** 3   **c)** 4   **d)** 5   **(1 mark)**

3 A dice is thrown and the scores are noted. The results are shown in the table below. What is the mean dice score? 📱

Dice score	1	2	3	4	5	6
Frequency	12	15	10	8	14	13

   a) 5   **b)** 3   **c)** 4   **d)** 3.5   **(1 mark)**

Score / 3

Short-answer questions

Answer all parts of each question.

1 Here are some number cards:

8	7	11	4	2	1	3	12	4	4

State whether the following statements, which refer to the number cards above, are **true** or **false**.

a) The range of the number cards is 1–11. .... **(1 mark)**

b) The mean of the number cards is 5.6 .... **(1 mark)**

c) The median of the number cards is 5. .... **(1 mark)**

d) The mode of the number cards is 4. .... **(1 mark)**

2 A baked beans factory claims, 'On average, a tin of baked beans contains 141 beans.'

In order to check the accuracy of this claim, a sample of 20 tins was taken and the number of beans in each tin counted.

Number of beans	137	138	139	140	141	142	143	144
Number of tins	1	1	1	2	5	4	4	2

a) Calculate the mean number of beans per tin. 📱 .... **(2 marks)**

b) Explain briefly whether you think the manufacturer is justified in making its claim.

.... **(1 mark)**

3 The mean of 7, 9, 10, 18, x and 17 is 13. What is the value of x? .... **(2 marks)**

Score / 9

Answer all parts of the questions. Show your workings (on a separate sheet of paper if necessary) and include the correct units in your answers.

1 Some students took a test. The table gives information about their marks in the test.

Mark	Frequency
3	2
4	5
5	11
6	2

a) Write down the modal mark. .... (1 mark)

b) Work out the range of the marks. .... (1 mark)

c) Work out the mean mark. 🔲

....

.... (3 marks)

2 Simon has sat three examinations. His mean score is 65. To pass the unit, he needs to get an average of 69. What score must he get in the fourth and final examination to pass the unit? 🔲

....

.... (3 marks)

3 A company employs three women and seven men. The mean weekly wage of the ten employees is £464. The mean weekly wage of the three women is £520. Calculate the mean weekly wage of the seven men. 🔲

....

.... (4 marks)

4 A magazine has 60 pages. The mean number of adverts per page for the whole magazine is 8. The mean number of adverts per page for the first 25 pages is 6. Calculate the mean number of adverts per page for the other 35 pages. 🔲

....

.... (3 marks)

Score   / 15

Statistics and probability

How well did you do?

| 0–9 | Try again | 10–15 | Getting there | 16–21 | Good work | 22–27 | Excellent! |

For more information on this topic, see pages 96–97 of your Success Revision Guide.

Averages 2

Multiple-choice questions

Choose just one answer, a, b, c or d. Circle your choice.

The following questions are based on the information given in the table opposite about the time taken by people to swim 50 metres.

Time t (seconds)	Frequency (f)
$0 \leqslant t < 30$	1
$30 \leqslant t < 60$	2
$60 \leqslant t < 90$	4
$90 \leqslant t < 120$	6
$120 \leqslant t < 150$	7
$150 \leqslant t < 180$	2

1 How many people swam 50 metres in less than 60 seconds?

   a) 2   **b)** 4

   c) 3   **d)** 6   **(1 mark)**

2 Which of the intervals is the modal class?

   a) $60 \leqslant t < 90$ **b)** $120 \leqslant t < 150$ **c)** $30 \leqslant t < 60$ **d)** $90 \leqslant t < 120$ **(1 mark)**

3 Which of the class intervals contains the median value?

   a) $90 \leqslant t < 120$ **b)** $150 \leqslant t < 180$ **c)** $120 \leqslant t < 150$ **d)** $60 \leqslant t < 90$ **(1 mark)**

4 What is the estimate for the mean time taken to swim 50 metres? 🖩

   a) 105 seconds   **b)** 385 seconds   **c)** 100 seconds   **d)** 125 seconds   **(1 mark)**

Score   / 4

Short-answer questions

Answer all parts of each question.

1 Information about the length of some seedlings is shown in the table opposite.

Calculate an estimate for the mean length of the seedlings.

Length L (mm)	Number of seedlings
$0 \leqslant L < 10$	3
$10 \leqslant L < 20$	5
$20 \leqslant L < 30$	9
$30 \leqslant L < 40$	2
$40 \leqslant L < 50$	1

Mean = _____ mm   **(4 marks)**

2 The stem-and-leaf diagram shows the marks gained by some students in a mathematics examination.

```
1 | 2 5 7
2 | 6 9
3 | 4 5 5 7
4 | 2 7 7 7 7
5 | 2
```

Using the stem-and-leaf diagram, work out...

   a) the mode _____   **(1 mark)**

   b) the median _____   **(1 mark)**

   c) the range. _____   Key: 1 | 2 = 12 marks   **(1 mark)**

Score   / 7

Answer all parts of the questions. Show your workings (on a separate sheet of paper if necessary) and include the correct units in your answers.

1 Some students did a logic problem. This back-to-back stem-and-leaf diagram shows how long they took, to the nearest minute, to complete the problem.

Boys' times		Girls' times
7 7 5 4 0	1	2 5 5 7
6 6 3 1 1	2	3 8 8 9
8 7	3	0 1 2 3 9
9 7 5	4	2 3

Key for boys' times: 7 | 1 = 17 minutes
Key for girls' times: 1 | 5 = 15 minutes

Compare and contrast the scores of the boys and the girls.

_____

_____ (4 marks)

2 Edward asks 100 people how much they spent last year on newspapers. The results are given in the table below.

Amount x (£)	Frequency
$0 \leqslant x < 10$	12
$10 \leqslant x < 20$	20
$20 \leqslant x < 30$	15
$30 \leqslant x < 40$	18
$40 \leqslant x < 50$	14
$50 \leqslant x < 60$	18
$60 \leqslant x < 70$	3

a) Calculate an estimate of the mean amount spent on newspapers. 🖩

_____ (4 marks)

b) Explain briefly why this value of the mean is only an estimate.

_____ (1 mark)

c) Calculate the class interval in which the median lies.

_____ (2 marks)

d) Edward claims, 'The average amount of money spent on newspapers last year was between £10 and £20.' Explain whether you think that Edward's claim is correct.

_____ (2 marks)

Score   / 13

How well did you do?

| 0–6 | Try again | 7–11 | Getting there | 12–17 | Good work | 18–24 | Excellent! |

For more information on this topic, see pages 98–99 of your Success Revision Guide.

Statistics and probability

Cumulative frequency graphs

Multiple-choice questions

Choose just one answer, a, b, c or d. Circle your choice.

The data below shows the number of letters delivered to each of the 15 houses in Whelan Avenue. Use this information to answer the following questions.
0, 0, 1, 1, 1, 1, 1, 1, 2, 2, 2, 3, 4, 5, 5

1 What is the median number of letters delivered?

   a) 0   **b)** 2   **c)** 1   **d)** 5   **(1 mark)**

2 What is the lower quartile for the number of letters delivered?

   a) 0   **b)** 2   **c)** 3   **d)** 1   **(1 mark)**

3 What is the interquartile range for the number of letters delivered?

   a) 2   **b)** 3   **c)** 4   **d)** 5   **(1 mark)**

Score   / 3

Short-answer questions

Answer all parts of each question.

1 The table shows the examination marks of some year 10 pupils in their end-of-year mathematics examination.

Examination mark	Frequency	Cumulative frequency
0–10	4	
11–20	6	
21–30	11	
31–40	24	
41–50	18	
51–60	7	
61–70	3	

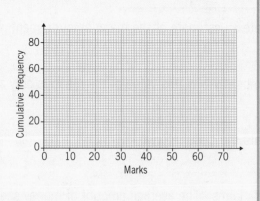

a) Complete the cumulative frequency column in the table above.   **(2 marks)**

b) Draw the cumulative frequency graph.   **(3 marks)**

c) From your graph, find the interquartile range. ....   **(2 marks)**

d) If 16 pupils were given a grade A in the examination, what is the minimum score needed for a grade A?

.... marks   **(2 marks)**

Score   / 9

Answer all parts of the questions. Show your workings (on a separate sheet of paper if necessary) and include the correct units in your answers.

1 The table shows the time, to the nearest minute, taken to run a marathon.

Time t (minutes)	Frequency	Cumulative frequency
$120 < t \leqslant 140$	1	
$140 < t \leqslant 160$	8	
$160 < t \leqslant 180$	24	
$180 < t \leqslant 200$	29	
$200 < t \leqslant 220$	10	
$220 < t \leqslant 240$	5	
$240 < t \leqslant 260$	3	

a) Complete the table to show the cumulative frequency for this data. (2 marks)

b) On a separate piece of graph paper, draw the cumulative frequency graph for this data. (3 marks)

c) Use your graph to work out an estimate for...

    i) the interquartile range .... minutes (2 marks)

    ii) the number of runners with a time of more than 205 minutes. .... (1 mark)

d) Draw a box plot for this data.

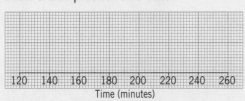

Time (minutes)

(3 marks)

e) The box plot below shows the times, to the nearest minute, taken to run another marathon two weeks later. Make two comparisons between the times taken to run the two marathons.

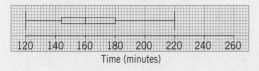

Time (minutes)

....

....

(2 marks)

Score   / 13

Statistics and probability

How well did you do?

| 0–6 | Try again | 7–12 | Getting there | 13–19 | Good work | 20–25 | Excellent! |

For more information on this topic, see pages 100–101 of your Success Revision Guide.

Histograms

Multiple-choice questions

Choose just one answer, a, b, c or d. Circle your choice.

The table shows the distance travelled to work by some employees. Use the information in the table to answer the questions below.

Distance d (km)	Frequency
$0 \leqslant d < 5$	8
$5 \leqslant d < 15$	20
$15 \leqslant d < 20$	135
$20 \leqslant d < 30$	47
$30 \leqslant d < 50$	80

1 Which class interval has a frequency density of 4.7?

  a) $0 \leqslant d < 5$ **b)** $5 \leqslant d < 15$

  c) $15 \leqslant d < 20$ **d)** $20 \leqslant d < 30$ (1 mark)

2 The frequency density for one of the class intervals is 4. Which one is it?

  a) $5 \leqslant d < 15$ **b)** $30 \leqslant d < 50$ **c)** $0 \leqslant d < 5$ **d)** $15 \leqslant d < 20$ (1 mark)

3 Which class interval has the **highest** frequency density?

  a) $0 \leqslant d < 5$ **b)** $15 \leqslant d < 20$ **c)** $20 \leqslant d < 30$ **d)** $5 \leqslant d < 15$ (1 mark)

4 Which class interval has the **lowest** frequency density?

  a) $0 \leqslant d < 5$ **b)** $5 \leqslant d < 15$ **c)** $15 \leqslant d < 20$ **d)** $30 \leqslant d < 50$ (1 mark)

Score / 4

Short-answer questions

Answer all parts of each question.

1 The table and histogram give information about how long, in minutes, some students took to complete a maths problem.

Time t (minutes)	Frequency
$0 < t \leqslant 5$	19
$5 < t \leqslant 15$	....
$15 < t \leqslant 20$	16
$20 < t \leqslant 30$	....
$30 < t \leqslant 45$	12

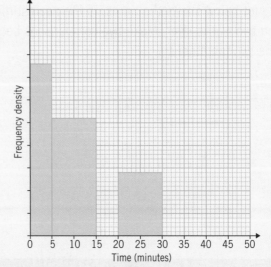

  a) Use the information in the histogram to complete the table.   (2 marks)

  b) Use the table to complete the histogram.   (2 marks)

Score / 4

GCSE-style questions

Answer all parts of the questions. Show your workings (on a separate sheet of paper if necessary) and include the correct units in your answers.

1 The masses of some objects are given in the table below.

Mass M (kg)	Frequency
$0 \leqslant M < 2$	14
$2 \leqslant M < 3$	8
$3 \leqslant M < 5$	13
$5 \leqslant M < 10$	14
$10 \leqslant M < 12$	7
$M \geqslant 12$	0

Draw a histogram to show the distribution of the mass of the objects. Use a scale of 1cm to 2kg on the mass axis.

(3 marks)

2 Pierre recorded the length, in seconds, of some advertisements shown on television in a week. His results are shown in the histogram.

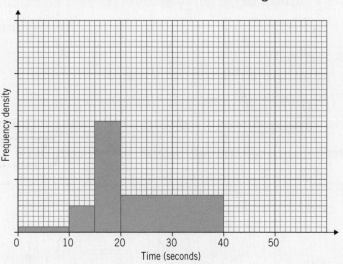

Time (seconds)

Use the information in the histogram to complete the table.

Time S (seconds)	Frequency
$0 \leqslant S < 10$	....
$10 \leqslant S < 15$	....
$15 \leqslant S < 20$	21
$20 \leqslant S < 40$	....
$S \geqslant 40$	0

(3 marks)

Score   / 6

How well did you do?

| 0–2 | Try again | 3–6 | Getting there | 7–10 | Good work | 11–14 | Excellent! |

For more information on this topic, see pages 93 and 102–103 of your Success Revision Guide.

Probability

Multiple-choice questions

Choose just one answer, a, b, c or d. Circle your choice.

1 The probability that Highbury football team wins a football match is $\frac{12}{17}$
What is the probability that the team does not win the football match?

a) $\frac{5}{12}$ **b)** $\frac{17}{29}$ **c)** $\frac{12}{17}$ **d)** $\frac{5}{17}$ (1 mark)

2 A fair dice is thrown 600 times. On how many of these throws would you expect to get a 4?

a) 40   **b)** 600   **c)** 100   **d)** 580   (1 mark)

3 A fair dice is thrown 500 times. If a 6 comes up 87 times, what is the relative frequency?

a) $\frac{1}{6}$ **b)** $\frac{87}{500}$ **c)** $\frac{10}{600}$ **d)** $\frac{1}{587}$ (1 mark)

4 The probability that it snows on Christmas Day is 0.2
What is the probability that it will snow on Christmas Day in two consecutive years?

a) 0.04   **b)** 0.4   **c)** 0.2   **d)** 0.16   (1 mark)

5 The probability that Fiona is in the hockey team is 0.7
The probability that she is picked for the netball team is 0.3
What is the probability that she is picked for both teams?

a) 1.0   **b)** 0.1   **c)** 0.12   **d)** 0.21   (1 mark)

Score   / 5

Short-answer questions

Answer all parts of each question.

1 Two spinners are spun at the same time and their scores are added. Drawing a sample space diagram or otherwise, find the probability of...

Spinner 1

3	3
2	1

Spinner 2

6	2
3	1

a) a score of 4 _____   (1 mark)

b) a score of 9 _____   (1 mark)

c) a score of 1 _____   (1 mark)

2 The probability that Michelle finishes first in a swimming race is 0.3
Michelle swims two races. Work out the probability that Michelle wins both races.

_____   (2 marks)

3 There are 13 counters in a bag: seven are red and the rest are white. A counter is picked at random, its colour noted and it is not replaced. A second counter is then chosen. What is the probability of choosing...

a) two red counters? _____   (2 marks)

b) a red and a white counter? _____   (3 marks)

Score   / 10

Answer all parts of the questions. Show your workings (on a separate sheet of paper if necessary) and include the correct units in your answers.

1 A bag contains different-coloured beads. The probability of taking a bead of a particular colour at random is as follows:

Colour	Red	White	Blue	Pink
Probability	0.25	0.1		0.3

Jackie is going to take a bead at random and then put it back in the bag.

a) i) Work out the probability that Jackie will take out a blue bead. _____ (1 mark)

   ii) Write down the probability that Jackie will take out a black bead. _____ (1 mark)

b) Jackie will take out a bead from the bag at random 200 times, replacing the bead each time. Work out an estimate for the number of times that Jackie takes a red bead.

_____ (2 marks)

2 Two fair dice are thrown together and their scores are added.

a) Work out the probability of a score of 7. _____ (2 marks)

b) Work out the probability of a score of 9. _____ (2 marks)

3 When driving to work, Zi Ying passes through two sets of traffic lights. If she stops at the first set of traffic lights, the probability that she stops at the second set of lights is 0.4. If she does not stop at the first set of traffic lights, the probability that she stops at the second set of lights is 0.3. The probability that Zi Ying stops at the first set of traffic lights is 0.2.

a) Draw a tree diagram to show this data in the space below.

(3 marks)

b) What is the probability that Zi Ying stops at only one set of traffic lights on her journey to work?

_____ (3 marks)

Score   / 14

How well did you do?

0–9 Try again   10–16 Getting there   17–23 Good work   24–29 Excellent!

For more information on this topic, see pages 104–107 of your Success Revision Guide.

Mixed GCSE-style questions

Answer these questions. Show full working out. Use a separate sheet of paper if necessary.

1 Katy sells CDs. She sells each CD for £9.20 plus VAT at 17.5%. She sells 127 CDs. Work out how much money Katy receives.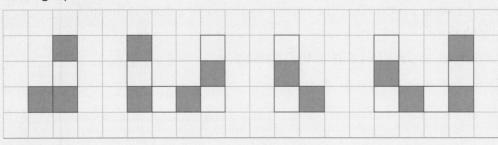

(4 marks)

2 Here is a diagram showing the side views of a model. The cubes are either blue or white.

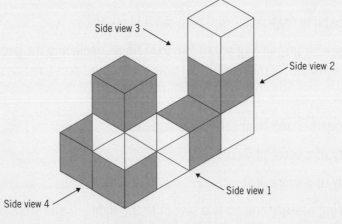

These drawings show the side views of the model. Write down which side view each drawing represents.

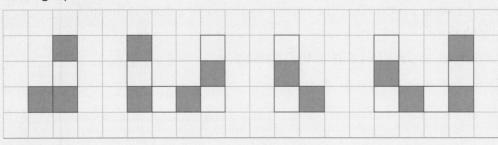

a) Side view _____ **b)** Side view _____ **c)** Side view _____ **d)** Side view _____

(2 marks)

3 Using a pair of compasses, bisect the angle XOY.

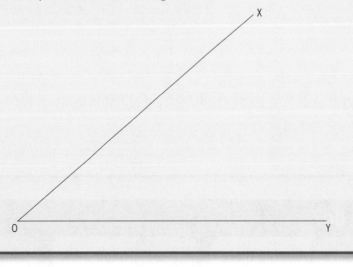

(3 marks)

④ The times, in minutes, taken by some students to finish an assault course are listed in order: 8, 12, 12, 13, 15, 17, 22, 23, 23, 27, 29

a) Find...

   i) the lower quartile   ....   (1 mark)

   ii) the interquartile range.   ....   (1 mark)

b) Draw a box plot for this data.

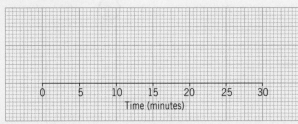

(3 marks)

c) A second group of students also do the assault course. The box plot of their times to complete the assault course is shown below.

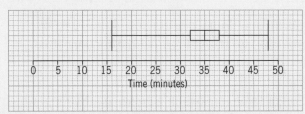

Make two comparisons of the times taken by each group of students to complete the assault course.

....

....   (2 marks)

⑤ The table gives the times to the nearest minute to complete a puzzle. Calculate an estimate for the mean number of minutes taken to complete the puzzle. 🖩

Time t (minutes)	Frequency
$0 \leqslant t < 10$	5
$10 \leqslant t < 20$	12
$20 \leqslant t < 30$	8
$30 \leqslant t < 40$	5

....

(4 marks)

⑥ The two frequency polygons show the heights of a group of year 7 girls and boys.

Compare the heights of the boys and the girls. Give a reason for your answer.

....

....   (3 marks)

7 Part of Mrs Allen's electricity bill is shown opposite. Work out the total cost of the electricity bill including VAT at 5%.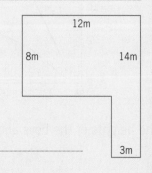

Electricity Bill	
New reading	11 427
Old reading	10 619
Cost per unit	12.5p

(4 marks)

8 Megan bought a TV for £700. Each year the value of the TV depreciated by 20%. Work out the value of the TV two years after she bought it.

(3 marks)

9 Estimate the value of $\dfrac{8.9 \times 5.2}{10.1}$

(2 marks)

10 a) Here are the first four terms of an arithmetic sequence: 5, 9, 13, 17, ...
Find an expression, in terms of n, for the nth term of the sequence.

(2 marks)

b) Here are the first four terms of an arithmetic sequence: 4, 10, 18, 28, ...
Find an expression, in terms of n, for the nth term of the sequence.

(2 marks)

11 The diagram shows the position of three markers in a cross-country race, which goes from A to B to C and directly back to A. AC is 10km. The bearing of A from C is 302°.

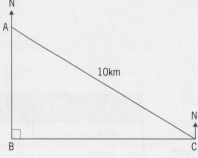

Work out the speed of an athlete who completes the race in 2 hours and 10 minutes. Give your answer to the nearest whole number.

(5 marks)

12 a) The number 360 can be written as $2^a \times 3^b \times 5^c$. Calculate the values of a, b and c.

(3 marks)

b) Find the highest common factor of 56 and 60. (2 marks)

c) Find the least common multiple of 56 and 60. (2 marks)

13 The diagram shows the plan of a garden. All the angles are right angles. Tracy wants to turf the garden. Turf costs £3.80 per square metre. You can only buy a whole number of square metres. Standard delivery cost is £17.50. How much will Tracy's turf cost, including delivery?

(5 marks)

14 Simplify the following:

a) $p^4 \times p^6$ ⟨blank⟩ (1 mark)

b) $\dfrac{p^7}{p^3}$ ⟨blank⟩ (1 mark)

c) $\dfrac{p^4 \times p^5}{p}$ ⟨blank⟩ (1 mark)

d) $(p^{-\frac{1}{2}})^4$ ⟨blank⟩ (1 mark)

15 $a = 2 + \sqrt{7}$ and $b = 2 - 3\sqrt{7}$

Simplify the following, giving your answer in the form $p + q\sqrt{7}$, where p and q are integers.

a) $a + b$ ⟨blank⟩ (3 marks)

b) a^2 ⟨blank⟩ (3 marks)

c) ab ⟨blank⟩ (3 marks)

16 The lines PQ and RS are parallel.

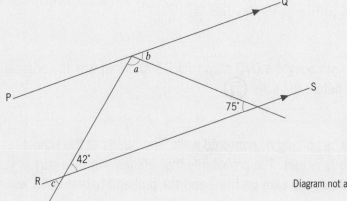

Diagram not accurately drawn

a) Write down the value of b. Give a reason for your answer.

⟨blank⟩ (2 marks)

b) Write down the value of c. Give a reason for your answer.

⟨blank⟩ (2 marks)

c) Write down the value of a. ⟨blank⟩ (2 marks)

17 a) Factorise $x^2 - 10x + 24$.

⟨blank⟩ (2 marks)

b) Hence solve $x^2 - 10x + 24 = 0$. ⟨blank⟩ (2 marks)

18 Simplify $\dfrac{x^2 + 2x}{x^2 + 5x + 6}$ ⟨blank⟩ (3 marks)

19 A, B and C are points on a circle, centre O.
Prove that the angle subtended by arc AC
at the centre of the circle is twice the angle
subtended by arc AC at point B.

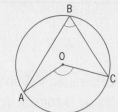

⟨blank⟩

⟨blank⟩ (4 marks)

20 The shape of a disused fish pond is a cylinder as shown. 1m³ of soil weighs 1.25 tonnes. A gardener wants to fill the pond with soil as cheaply as possible. The table shows the cost that two companies charge to do this.

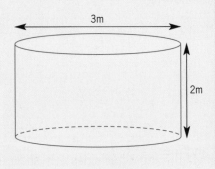

3m

2m

Goodgrow Soil	£52 per tonne	Delivery £25
Super Soil	7 tonnes for £340, then £68.25 per extra tonne	Free delivery

Which company should the gardener use and how much will it cost?

_____

_____ **(6 marks)**

21 a) Solve $5x - 2 = 3(x + 6)$ $x =$ _____ **(2 marks)**

b) Solve $\frac{3 - 2x}{4} = 2$ $x =$ _____ **(2 marks)**

22 Prove that $0.6\overset{..}{2}\overset{.}{9}$ can be written as the fraction $\frac{623}{990}$

_____ **(2 marks)**

23 In a '20% off' sale, William bought a DVD player for £300. What was the original price of the DVD player before the sale? 🖩

_____ **(3 marks)**

24 Riddlington High School is holding a sponsored walk. The pupils at the school decide whether or not to take part. The probability that Afshan will take part is $\frac{2}{3}$. The probability that Bethany will take part is $\frac{4}{5}$ and the probability that Colin will take part is $\frac{1}{4}$

Calculate the probability that...

a) all three take part in the sponsored walk

_____ **(2 marks)**

b) two of them take part in the sponsored walk.

_____ **(3 marks)**

25 a) $b = \frac{a + c}{ac}$ $a = 3.2 \times 10^5$ $c = 5 \times 10^6$

Calculate the value of b.
Give your answer in standard form. 🖩 _____ **(2 marks)**

b) Rearrange the formula to make a the subject. _____ **(2 marks)**

26 This is the formula used for changing degrees Fahrenheit (F) into degrees centigrade (C):

$C = \frac{5(F - 32)}{9}$

In August, the average temperature in Dubai is 43°C. Maisie says that this is over 100°F. Decide whether Maisie is correct. You must show sufficient working to justify your answer. 🖩

_____ **(3 marks)**

27 a) p is an integer such that $0 < 4p \leqslant 13$. List all the possible values of p.

(1 mark)

b) Solve the inequality $\frac{t+1}{4} \leqslant t - 3$.

(2 marks)

28 Prove that $(3t + 1)^2 - (3t - 1)^2$ is a multiple of 4 for all positive values of t.

(3 marks)

29 The right-angled triangle has sides x, y and $x + 1$. x and y are integers.

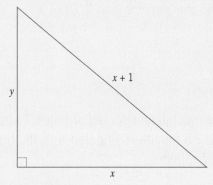

Prove that y must be an odd number.

(5 marks)

30 PQRS is a cyclic quadrilateral.
PS = 4.3cm, SR = 2.7cm, angle
PSR = 143° and PQ = QR.

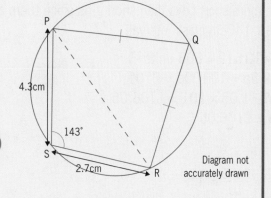

a) Calculate the length of PR.

_____ cm

(3 marks)

b) Calculate the area of triangle PQR.

_____ cm²

Diagram not accurately drawn

(6 marks)

31 Solve the equation $\frac{x-4}{x^2-16} + \frac{2}{2x-4} = 1$

Leave your answers in surd form.　　$x =$ _____ or $x =$ _____

(5 marks)

32 The diagram shows a child's toy, which is hollow. The toy is made of a cone and hemisphere. The height of the cone is 4cm. The base radius of the cone and hemisphere is 3cm.

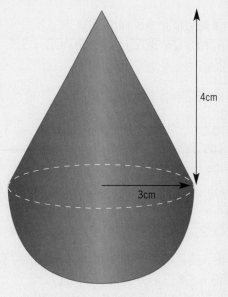

a) Work out the total surface area of the toy. Give your answer as a multiple of π.

_____ cm²

(4 marks)

b) The toy is made in two sizes. The large toy is three times the size of the toy opposite. What is the total surface area of the large toy? Give your answer as a multiple of π.

_____ cm²

Diagram not accurately drawn

(3 marks)

1 9.20 × 1.175 = £10.81 with VAT for each CD.
127 × £10.81 = £1372.87

2 a) Side view 4   **b)** Side view 1   **c)** Side view 2   **d)** Side view 3

3 Construction lines should be shown and the bisector is at 20° (±1°).

4 a) i) 12   **ii)** 11
   b)

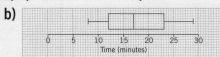

   c) The second group of students has a much larger spread of times. In general, they are slower as their median time was 35 minutes compared with the first group of students whose median time was 17 minutes.

5 19.3̇ minutes

6 The girls are generally taller than the boys. There are more tall girls than tall boys, since there are 4 girls in the 160–165cm class interval compared with only 1 boy. There are more short boys than short girls since there are 3 boys and only 1 girl in the 135–140cm class interval.

7 11 427 – 10 619 = 808 units
808 × 12.5p = 10 100p = £101
VAT @ 5%: 1.05 × 101 = £106.05
Total bill = £106.05

8 £448

9 $\dfrac{8.9 \times 5.2}{10.1} \approx \dfrac{9 \times 5}{10} = 4.5$

10 a) $4n + 1$
    b) $n^2 + 3n$

11 Calculate the length of AB and BC.
Bearing of A from C = 302°, so angle ACB = 32°.
$\text{Sin } 32° = \dfrac{AB}{10}$
AB = 10 × sin 32° = 5.3km
$\text{Cos } 32° = \dfrac{BC}{10}$
BC = 10 × cos 32° = 8.48km
Total distance = 23.78km
$s = \dfrac{d}{t} = \dfrac{23.78}{2\frac{10}{60}} = 10.975... = 11\text{km/h}$

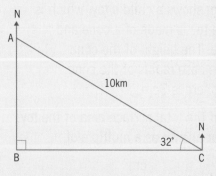

12 a) $a = 3, b = 2, c = 1$ **b)** 4   **c)** 840

13 Area of garden: 12 × 8 = 96m², 6 × 3 = 18m², Total = 114m²
      114 × £3.80 = £433.20, delivery = £17.50
      Total cost = £433.20 + £17.50 = £450.70

14 a) p^{10} **b)** p^4 **c)** p^8 **d)** $p^{-2} = \dfrac{1}{p^2}$

15 a) $4 - 2\sqrt{7}$ **b)** $11 + 4\sqrt{7}$ **c)** $-17 - 4\sqrt{7}$

16 a) $b = 75°$ since angle b and $75°$ are alternate angles.
     b) $c = 42°$ since angle c and $42°$ are vertically opposite.
     c) $a = 63°$

17 a) $(x - 4)(x - 6)$ **b)** $x = 4$ and $x = 6$

18 $\dfrac{x(x + 2)}{(x + 2)(x + 3)} = \dfrac{x}{x + 3}$

19 To prove angle AOC = 2 × angle ABC:
Draw the line BO and produce it to D.
OA = OC = OB since all are radii.
Triangle OAB is isosceles,
so angle OAB and OBA = x.
Triangle OBC is isosceles,
so angle OBC and angle OCB = y.
Since angle BOA = $180° - 2x$
then angle AOD = $2x$.
Since angle BOC = $180° - 2y$
then angle DOC = $2y$.
Hence the angle AOC = 2 × angle ABC

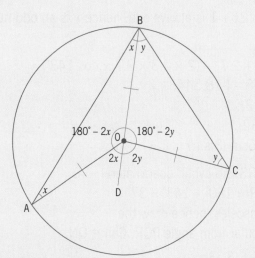

20 Volume of pond = $\pi \times r^2 \times h = \pi \times 1.5^2 \times 2 = 14.14\text{m}^3$
$14.14 \times 1.25 = 17.67 \therefore 18$ tonnes of soil are needed.
Goodgrow Soil: $52 \times 18 + 25 = £961$
Super Soil: $340 + (11 \times 68.25) = £1090.75$
$\therefore$ the gardener should use Goodgrow Soil at £961.

21 a) $x = 10$ **b)** $x = -2.5$

22 Let $x = 0.629\ 292\ 9\ldots$
$10x = 6.292\ 929\ldots$
$1000x = 629.292\ 929\ldots$
$1000x - 10x = 629.292\ 929\ldots - 6.292\ 929\ldots$
$990x = 623$
$x = \frac{623}{990}$, hence $0.6\dot{2}\dot{9} = \frac{623}{990}$

23 £375

24 The use of a tree diagram will help you to answer this question.

     a) $\frac{2}{15}$ **b)** $\frac{1}{2}$

25 a) 3.325×10^{-6} **b)** $a = \dfrac{c}{bc - 1}$

26 $C = \dfrac{5(F - 32)}{9}$

     $C = \dfrac{5 \times (100 - 32)}{9} = 37.\dot{7}$

     Since $100°F = 37.\dot{7}°C$, a temperature of $43°C$ must be greater than $100°F$,
     so Maisie is correct.

27 a) $1, 2, 3$

     b) $t \geqslant \frac{13}{3}$

28 $(3t + 1)^2 - (3t - 1)^2$
$[(3t + 1)(3t + 1)] - [(3t - 1)(3t - 1)]$
$[(9t^2 + 6t + 1) - (9t^2 - 6t + 1)]$
$= 12t$
Since 12 is a multiple of 4, then $12t$ is a multiple of 4 for all positive values of t.

29 $x^2 + y^2 = (x + 1)^2$
$x^2 + y^2 = (x + 1)(x + 1)$
$x^2 + y^2 = x^2 + 2x + 1$
$y^2 = 2x + 1$
$2x$ is even so $2x + 1$ is always odd, hence y is an odd number.

30 a) Call PR, x:
$x^2 = 4.3^2 + 2.7^2 - (2 \times 4.3 \times 2.7 \times \cos 143°)$
$x^2 = 25.78 - (-18.5443...)$
$x^2 = 44.32...$
$x = \sqrt{44.32...}$
PR = 6.66cm (3 s.f.)

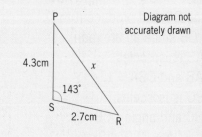
Diagram not accurately drawn

b) Since PQRS is a cyclic quadrilateral,
angle PQR = $180° - 143° = 37°$
PQR is isosceles, hence draw the
perpendicular from angle PQR. Call it QN.

$\text{Tan } 18.5° = \dfrac{3.33}{QN}$

$QN = \dfrac{3.33}{\tan 18.5°}$

$QN = 9.95$cm

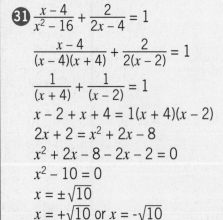

Area of PQR = $\frac{1}{2} \times 6.66 \times 9.95$
$= 33.1$cm^2 (3 s.f.)

31 $\dfrac{x - 4}{x^2 - 16} + \dfrac{2}{2x - 4} = 1$

$\dfrac{x - 4}{(x - 4)(x + 4)} + \dfrac{2}{2(x - 2)} = 1$

$\dfrac{1}{(x + 4)} + \dfrac{1}{(x - 2)} = 1$

$x - 2 + x + 4 = 1(x + 4)(x - 2)$
$2x + 2 = x^2 + 2x - 8$
$x^2 + 2x - 8 - 2x - 2 = 0$
$x^2 - 10 = 0$
$x = \pm\sqrt{10}$
$x = +\sqrt{10}$ or $x = -\sqrt{10}$

32 a) Curved surface area of cone = πrl
$\pi \times 3 \times 5 = 15\pi$
Curved surface area of hemisphere = $\dfrac{4\pi r^2}{2}$
$2\pi \times 9 = 18\pi$
Total curved surface area = 33π cm^2

b) Linear scale factor = 3
Area scale factor = $3^2 = 9$
Curved surface area of larger toy = 297π cm^2